WALL OF SILENCE

THE PECULIAR MURDER OF
JIM DAWSON
AT BASHALL EAVES

JENNIFER LEE COBBAN

Demdike Press, 2005

Wall of Silence
Jennifer Lee Cobban

First Edition

Published by Demdike Press, 2005

Copyright © J. L. Cobban, 2005

ALL RIGHTS RESERVED

No part of this publication may be reproduced, stored in a retrieval system, or transmitted in any form or by any means mechanical, electronic, photocopying or otherwise, without the prior permission of the publisher.

Cover Illustration © Annabel Spenceley, 2005

Demdike Press,
3 Beech Grove, Chatburn, BB7 4AR

Printed by Lloyds Printers of Blackburn Ltd.

ISBN No: 0-9550437-0-0

Published by Demdike Press

This book is dedicated to my Great-uncle,

JAMES DAWSON OF BASHALL HALL
1887 – 1934

*who was shot by an unknown assailant
on Sunday 18th March, 1934*

R.I.P.

Contents

Photos and Illustrations: .... *Page 6*
About the Author: .... *Page 7*
Acknowledgements: .... *Page 8*
Introduction: .... *Page 9*

PART ONE: THE LIFE AND DEATH OF JIM DAWSON .... *Page 15*

Chapter 1:   The Shadow of the Talbots .... *Page 17*
Chapter 2:   The Dawsons of Bashall Hall .... *Page 27*
Chapter 3:   Prelude to Murder, 1933-34 .... *Page 46*
Chapter 4:   The Murder .... *Page 65*
Chapter 5:   'No Development, No Clue, No Motive": .... *Page 80*
              The Murder Investigation

PART 2:   THE QUEST FOR THE TRUTH .... *Page 99*

Chapter 6:   Seeking the Ghost of Jim Dawson .... *Page 101*
              and the Missing Case File
Chapter 7:   Bashall Eaves and the Wall of Silence: .... *Page 113*
              Theories Old and New
Chapter 8:   Final Thoughts, a Hidden Gun and .... *Page 129*
              a Deathbed Confession (?)

Appendix 1:   Significant Dates in the Life and Death of Jim Dawson .... *Page 145*
Appendix 2:   Postscript .... *Page 149*
Appendix 3:   Dawson Family Tree .... *Page 154*
Sources   .... *Page 156*
Other places to visit .... *Page 160*

Photos and Illustrations

1. Clitheroe looking towards Pendle Hill .... *Page 11*
2. Fairy Bridge, Bashall Eaves .... *Page 11*
3. Peg o' Nell at Waddow Hall .... *Page 19*
4. The 'relics' of Henry VI .... *Page 19*
5. Simplified Dawson Family Tree .... *Page 29*
6. The Dawson family at Bashall Hall .... *Page 30*
7. Bashall Eaves School .... *Page 31*
8. Matthew Dawson's school book .... *Page 31*
9. Charles Dawson, (Jim Dawson's uncle) .... *Page 33*
10. The bridge over Bashall Brook .... *Page 34*
11. Jim Dawson, the murder victim .... *Page 37*
12. Annie Dawson, (Jim Dawson's sister) .... *Page 39*
13. Tommy Kenyon, farmhand at Bashall Hall .... *Page 49*
14. The Dawson and Simpson ladies .... *Page 50*
15. John Dawson, (Jim Dawson's brother) .... *Page 52*
16. Advertisement for Bashall Eaves Show, 1933 .... *Page 53*
17. Bashall Hall in 1934 .... *Page 56*
18. The gazebo at Bashall Hall .... *Page 57*
19. 'The Barracks', Bashall Hall, 1934 .... *Page 59*
20. 'The Barracks', Bashall Hall, about 1980 .... *Page 59*
21. The Edisford Bridge Inn .... *Page 63*
22. Location map of area .... *Page 66*
23. The Murder Scene: Back Lane .... *Page 70*
24. The Murder Scene: Brieryforth Gate .... *Page 70*
25. Polly Pickles, (Jim Dawson's sister) .... *Page 73*
26. Lily Lee, (Jim Dawson's sister) .... *Page 73*
27. Harry Dawson (Jim Dawson's brother) .... *Page 76*
28. Harry Dawson at Waddington .... *Page 76*
29. Jim Dawson's grave at Mitton church .... *Page 85*
30. Albert Pickles dipping sheep, Bashall Brook .... *Page 87*
31. Henry Bleazard and Jim Lambert, Bashall Brook .... *Page 87*
32. Bob Dawson (Jim Dawson's brother) .... *Page 89*
33. Jack Lee, (Jim Dawson's nephew) .... *Page 94*
34. Albert Pickles, (Jim Dawson's nephew) .... *Page 94*
35. Bashall Town, the Simpson farm .... *Page 124*
36. The Wedding of Nancy Simpson .... *Page 126*

About the Author

JENNIFER Lee Cobban was brought up in Whalley, Lancashire and attended Clitheroe Royal Grammar School for Girls before gaining a degree from Manchester University in Ancient History and Archaeology. She has worked in television, public relations and teaching. After moving to North London in 1983, she spent almost 20 years helping to run Barnet Museum as Archaeology Officer and acting as a liaison point between local heritage groups and English Heritage. Jennifer returned to the Ribble Valley in 2002 and now lives near Clitheroe.

Her particular interests and specialist knowledge include the history and archaeology of witchcraft and folk magic and the history of the Knights Templar. She also enjoys the cinema, television, gardening and chasing ghosts about.

Her first book, *Geoffrey de Mandeville and London's Camelot: Ghosts, Mysteries and the Occult in Barnet* was published in 1997 and her second, *800 Years of Barnet Market* (with Doreen Willcocks) was published in 1999.

Acknowledgements

I WOULD like to thank North Yorkshire Police for all its help and for allowing me to consult the murder file of Jim Dawson. Particular thanks are due to Chief Constable Della Cannings, Inspector Richard Spedding, and Christina Scaife of North Yorkshire Information Compliance Unit.

I am also extremely grateful to all the staff of Clitheroe Library - particularly Mrs. Sue Holden of Clitheroe Library Local Studies, without whose expertise I would have found myself well and truly lost. Sue very kindly placed her extensive local knowledge at my disposal throughout the writing of the book.

Thanks are also due to my father Mr. J. G. Lee for the family photos, family tree and personal memories of the events of 1934 and also to Annabel Spenceley for providing the cover illustration.

Others who deserve particular mention are Detective Chief Superintendent Paul Buschini and D.S. Proctor of Lancashire Constabulary, The Clitheroe Advertiser and Times, Sir Max Hastings, Stan Stuart, Don Masters, Nick Cobban, J. S. Bailey, Gertrude Hird, Skipton Museum and Library, the Universities of Boston and Texas, Abingdon Historical and Archaeological Society and Ken Ward.

And last but not least, thanks to all those who chose to remain anonymous.

While many people have helped with the research for this book by making information available to me, I must make it clear that they might not necessarily agree with the use to which I have put this information. Any misinterpretations and mistakes are entirely my own.

Every attempt has been made to obtain permission for the use of all quotations and illustrations, but in a couple of cases it has proved impossible to contact the copyright holder. Any omissions notified to the author will of course be rectified in any future editions of the book.

Introduction

IN March 1934 the residents of a sleepy rural village called Bashall Eaves were stunned by news of the bizarre murder of a well-known local farmer. The murder victim was my great-uncle Jim Dawson of Bashall Hall, a manor house lying a couple of miles from Bashall Eaves village, near Clitheroe in Lancashire. The mystery of how he died, and why, has never been solved. Some have even dubbed it, "The Perfect Crime".

Although it is more than 70 years since he was shot by an unknown assailant on a lonely country lane, the crime remains a curiously touchy subject in the Clitheroe area resulting in continuous media interest and much local gossip and speculation.

A television documentary on the case in 1964 asserted that Bashall Eaves was not only a close-knit community, but a backward one where the villagers treated people who came from ten miles away as foreigners. A second TV programme in 1979 labelled them tight-lipped and unhelpful and christened Bashall Eaves "The Village That Wouldn't Talk". Local residents were even accused of throwing up a 'wall of silence' to shield the truth about the crime from the investigating officers. How information contained within these TV programmes continues to contaminate genuine local memory of the event is an interesting issue and will later be analysed in some detail.

The strange crime happened on the dark, wet and windy night of March 18th 1934. At around nine p.m. Jim Dawson, a mild-mannered 46-year-old bachelor farmer, downed his last few drops of Duttons ale, bought a box of matches and left the Edisford Bridge Hotel near Clitheroe, where he had spent an apparently quiet and uneventful evening drinking and chatting with other local farmers.

It was a good 20 minute walk back to his home, the imposing medieval manor house of Bashall Hall. After fifteen minutes or so walking along the Clitheroe Road, Jim arrived at the entrance to Back Lane, a narrow road leading to Bashall Town Farm where his friend and neighbour Tommy Simpson lived and, eventually, home. A couple of minutes earlier he had noticed, by the lights of two oncoming cars, a man standing by the gate opposite the entrance to the lane. By the time Jim arrived there, however, the man had disappeared.

After walking a few yards along the dark and apparently deserted Back Lane, Jim Dawson heard what he later described as a click and immediately afterwards felt a sharp sting in his right shoulder. Believing that someone was playing a joke and had thrown a stone at him, he didn't look back but carried on walking.

Jim arrived home at 9.20 p.m. He had a good supper and retired to bed without saying a word about the incident to his relatives. He did not realise it, but a huge bullet was lodged in his shoulder.

On the following morning, Jim Dawson attended a private radiologist, and an X-ray revealed the truth of the matter. However, rather than have the bullet removed there and then, he made the surprising decision to refuse all medical treatment, insisting instead on returning home to Bashall Hall. As a result, the bullet wound became infected and he died of septicaemia in a Blackburn nursing home four days later on the 22nd March 1934. He never changed his original police statement that he did not know who had fired the fatal shot.

The murder of Jim Dawson of Bashall Hall should have been solved in a matter of days. It looked like a straightforward case, for in such a sparsely populated area there were relatively few suspects.

But as the investigation into this bizarre killing dragged on week after week, it became increasingly obvious that Chief Superintendent Blacker of the West Riding Constabulary was baffled. The case seemed to have as many false trails and red herrings as an Agatha Christie novel. It wasn't just that the investigating officers failed to find the murderer. In spite of the assistance of Robert Churchill, the country's top independent ballistics expert, the police were unable to decide whether the fateful shot had been fired from a gun or from some other kind of weapon, such as a powerful catapult. Blacker and Churchill were also extremely puzzled by the bullet which had been removed from Jim Dawson's body - it was made of steel, was unusually large and had the appearance of being home-made.

The motive was equally perplexing. Jim Dawson seemed to be universally popular and was apparently without an enemy in the world. Nobody had a word to say against him. Initially, he appeared to have little interest in women, or indeed in anything else much apart from running the Bashall Hall estate.

The open verdict recorded by the Blackburn Coroner three months later says it all. Jim Dawson may have been murdered, but then again he might have been killed by accident or in mistake for another man. The police, however, were always convinced that it was a case of murder and his family agreed with them. It remains open today as a classic 'cold case'.

Far from being the simple case it had at first appeared, its perplexing aspects have proved an irresistible challenge for amateur detectives and criminologists in the years since it happened, dozens of whom have struggled to solve the puzzle. But without success. Mystified, these investigators have dubbed the case anything from "one of the most remarkable puzzles in criminal history" to "the greatest murder mystery of the twentieth century".

The village of Bashall Eaves, where Jim Dawson lived out his ill-fated life, has changed very little since 1934. At that time it was part of Yorkshire, but was unceremoniously shifted into Lancashire during local government reorganisation in

The market town of Clitheroe circa 1950, taken from the castle keep looking west towards Pendle Hill. *Photo: Courtesy of Clitheroe Library*

The picturesque sixteenth-century Fairy Bridge (also known as Saddle Bridge) in Bashall Eaves, said to have been built overnight by the little people. The present proximity of electric fences to the bridge has probably seen to it that any passing fairies have been burnt to a crisp. *Photo: Clitheroe Library, courtesy of Pye's of Clitheroe*

April 1974. It remains merely a tiny village on the road from the bustling market town of Clitheroe, with its up-market shops and delightful castle, to the wild and romantic tourist destination of the Trough of Bowland. The village of Dunsop Bridge in the Forest of Bowland is reckoned to be the nearest village to the exact centre of the British Isles and it is maintained that the Queen has expressed a desire to retire to this beautiful region.

The nearest large population centres are Manchester (about an hour's drive away to the south west) and the old industrial towns of Blackburn and Burnley, both about eleven miles distant. However, the Bashall Eaves and Clitheroe area has about as much in common with industrial towns as sunlight has with soot.

For the countryside in which Bashall Eaves and Clitheroe nestle is everyone's idea of the typical rural idyll. Set in the green and fertile Ribble Valley, the scattered communities are protected by the rolling hills which surround them, including the impressive bulk of the bewitched and bewitching Pendle Hill to the west. The landscape has an unspoiled beauty which the ravage of centuries has done very little to alter.

Nothing much changes in the Ribble Valley. Even in the 21st century it remains a conservative and superstitious area steeped in myth and legend. It is from this magical countryside that J. R. R. Tolkien is thought to have derived inspiration for "The Shire". He is believed to have written some sections of "The Lord of the Rings" trilogy while staying with his son at Stonyhurst College, near the village of Hurst Green, between 1942 and 1947. The picturesque hill called Kemple End, upon which Jim Dawson gazed every day as he walked home from the Edisford Bridge Hotel, has been identified with Tolkien's Woody End. Mitton Wood has been equated with The Old Forest, while Hurst Green itself is rumoured to be his role model for Hobbiton, where Frodo and Sam lived their lives of bucolic bliss before embarking on their perilous journey to Mordor and Mount Doom.

Clitheroe, which is the nearest town to Bashall Eaves, is famously said to have one foot planted in Lancashire while the other rests very firmly in fairyland. The fairy folk are also to be found at the picturesque Fairy Bridge in Bashall Eaves. According to legend, this sixteenth century bridge was erected overnight by fairies to help out an old woodcutter who was being bullied by a witch (always a risk in this area!).

Strange witch stones are to be found on many old farm buildings - serving as an historical reminder of the superstitious fear generated by the trial of the famous Pendle Witches, as a result of which several local people were hanged for their so-called crimes on Lancaster Moor in 1612.

King Arthur even gets a look in - local legend tells of a battle he fought in the vicinity of Jim Dawson's home, Bashall Hall.

There are haunted locations in abundance. Indeed it is difficult to find any pub, river or private house in the area which does not boast an associated ghost story. The Punch Bowl at Hurst Green is haunted by the ghost of a highwayman, Ned King, while Peg O' Nell lurks by the River Ribble at Brungerley, impatient for human or animal sacrifice. Recent stories even maintain that the ghost of Jim Dawson haunts Bashall Eaves as a misshapen figure forever searching the hedges in Back Lane for the weapon that fired the deadly bullet. Bashall Hall itself is said to be haunted by the phantom of a medieval king.

This wonderful old building lies approximately two miles from the village of Bashall Eaves on the Clitheroe side, and is hidden from view by a slight rise in the ground. Built by the warlike Talbot family in the fifteenth century, the hall has a violent and bloody history. Family tradition has it that King Henry VI, who placed an undying curse upon the Talbot family during the Wars of the Roses, haunts the manor house. It seems a fitting place for a murder victim to have lived out his life. The Dawsons had occupied the old Talbot home as tenant farmers since the late eighteenth century. The family's connection with the estate was eventually severed in 1972 when Bashall Hall was sold by its owners, the Worsley-Taylor family.

As a result of media interest in the case, along with the presence of his ghost story in books about paranormal occurrences in the North West, accurate information concerning the murder of my great-uncle Jim Dawson today seems in imminent danger of being submerged beneath a welter of misconception and legend-building. I have nothing whatsoever against ghost stories and legends per se, having investigated and published on such subjects myself. However, little excuse can be found for playing fast and loose with readily checkable facts in such a well-documented case.

As researchers copy each others' mistakes, errors and inaccuracies have slowly but inexorably crept into his story. So-called facts about the case offered to television companies by unreliable witnesses with faulty memories (or with something to hide) have been accepted and repeated as the truth.

Indeed the situation has reached the point where accounts of the event have become so contaminated by careless errors and pure invention that it is difficult to believe that the murder of Jim Dawson was an actual historical event rather than just another local fairy story.

In the growing hype, some people also seem to have lost sight of the fact that Jim Dawson was essentially a man with normal human feelings, hopes and aspirations who left behind a family who mourned him in 1934 and continues to do so today.

While it is understood, then, that any unsolved murder is the stuff legends are made of, the murder of Jim Dawson is essentially an historical event and can be studied as such, using conventional historical tools and methodology. We should remember that Jim's story did not begin and end in March 1934. No incident can be examined in isolation from its historical context.

In order to be able to understand Jim Dawson's personal circumstances on March 18th 1934, I therefore decided it would be valuable to inform the reader fully about what had happened to Jim and his family and friends in the years before the murder itself took place. In this way, the account of the murder and its investigation should hopefully be far more readily understandable as the individuals concerned in these dramatic events will already be familiar. It would also offer readers the opportunity to come up with their own potential solutions to the crime if they felt inclined to do so. What follows is therefore something of a unusual family saga. It chronicles the full tragic history of a murder victim, his family and his ancestral home.

Having familiarised ourselves with the personalities involved, we can then move onto a detailed description of the murder itself, and the conduct of the murder investigation, using source material which has hitherto been unavailable to the general public. As Jim Dawson's great-niece, I found myself in the unique position of being granted unprecedented access to the original murder file, now lodged with the North Yorkshire Police. The story of my long and frustrating quest to locate this file and the exhibits relating to the murder of Jim Dawson is related here in full.

Also utilised in painting a vivid picture of the events of 1934 are family memories, archives and photographs. My father, Jack Lee, who was sleeping in the same bedroom as his Uncle Jim on the night of the murder, has for the first time agreed to the publication of his personal memories about that fateful night. He has also provided a mass of detail about how life was lived at Bashall Hall in the early 1930s. Much hitherto inaccessible information about the case is thus presented to the public for the first time.

Numerous other sources have been drawn upon to present a full account of the Jim Dawson case, including newspaper accounts of the time, interviews with Jim's friends and acquaintances and a recent appeal for information through the local newspapers. Many of those responding to the appeal chose to remain anonymous for one reason or another. As previously indicated, the murder of Jim Dawson remains a notoriously controversial subject, and local residents are not yet entirely prepared to abandon their infamous "wall of silence". Just as Jim's relatives continue to reside and work in the Clitheroe area, it is a fair bet that friends and relatives of the murderer are still living nearby. No doubt they watch and wait apprehensively for the day the killer's identity is finally revealed to the world.

"Wall of Silence" is the story of a tragic family spanning well over two centuries of history and legend, and is also a detailed examination of one of the most bizarre puzzles in the annals of criminology. Its aim is to restore humanity to the ever-evolving myth that has become Jim Dawson. This book is dedicated to his memory.

PART ONE

THE LIFE AND DEATH OF JIM DAWSON

CHAPTER 1

The Shadow of the Talbots

JIM Dawson was born in 1887 at Bashall Hall, an imposing stone manor house lying about two miles south of Bashall Eaves village, near Clitheroe in Lancashire. In days past, family feuds and civil disorder were common occurrences in this remote and often lawless corner of England on the Lancashire/Yorkshire borders. The most illustrious and notorious residents of Bashall Hall in medieval times were members of the Talbot family, who throughout their history had been experts in the art of murder and political manoeuvring. The subsequent history of the hall suggests that their bloody deeds might well have soaked into the very fabric of the ground on which the hall stood, producing a malign influence on the lives of many of its future residents.

We can imagine the shades of the Talbots and their victims hovering restlessly around the ancient manor house as this future murder victim made his entrance into the world.

★ ★ ★ ★ ★ ★ ★ ★ ★

Bashall, (originally Baschelf), lying within the parish of Great Mitton, is thought to mean 'the slope by the brook'. The name appears to contain a Viking element. It is first mentioned in the Domesday survey of 1086 as a former possession of Earl Tostig, the brother of King Harold. At that time settlement in the area consisted of scattered farmsteads (much as is does today), the main nucleus probably focusing upon the present Bashall Town, which lies very close to Bashall Hall. It has been observed that modern visitors are bemused by the name, expecting to find a substantial community and finding instead only a cluster of farm buildings*. In fact 'Town' in this case is merely a relatively modern corruption of the Old English word 'ton' (or farm). Bashall 'ton' may perhaps have been a more extensive settlement in earlier days, but without extensive archaeological survey and excavation it is impossible to be certain. The other main settlement was in all likelihood on the site of the present Bashall Eaves village some two miles distant, whose name indicates that it was on the 'eaves', or edge, of the royal hunting estate known as the Forest of Bowland.

William the Conqueror handed over Earl Tostig's Manor of Grindleton (which included Bashall) to his supporter Roger de Poiteau. However by 1101 Roger's estates had in turn been confiscated and granted instead to the De Lacy family, whose

---

* One of the farm buildings, Bashall Barn, has been converted into a local craft centre. Excellent food and drink are available in the café upstairs, and there is ample parking.

members became the Earls of Lincoln through marriage in 1232. The influential De Lacy family relied upon the support of hundreds of supporters (or retainers), to maintain its power and prestige. Among those brought from Lincolnshire to the De Lacy fee of Pontefract were members of the Talbot family, who probably settled in the area around the Bowland Forest soon after 1232.

In 1253, Edmund de Lacy granted the manor of Bashall to Thomas Talbot, a former Constable of Clitheroe Castle, for an annual payment of £8-10s-7d. Edmund Talbot, his son, gradually purchased properties in the area from local families, amongst whom were the Singletons of Withgill, near Mitton. By 1304 he had acquired most of the available land within the manor. In the same year he was knighted, and granted free warren (sole hunting rights) within his demesne lands. The Talbot family had become a force to be reckoned with. It is likely that work on the construction of a suitable manor house, befitting the family's enhanced station in life, commenced at around this time.

The Talbots Capture King Henry VI

By the mid-fifteenth century the country was in chaos as a result of the Wars of the Roses. During this conflict the armies of the Lancastrian king Henry VI, and of the Yorkist Edward IV, struggled for supremacy for over thirty years. This is not the place to go into the exceptionally complex politics of the time. Suffice it to say that the Talbot family supported the Yorkist cause. This caused tension in the Great Mitton area because the powerful Singleton clan at nearby Withgill, from whom the Talbots had acquired land within the manor of Bashall, appear to have supported the Lancastrian cause.

Both families had scores of relatives and servants to call upon in times of strife. (A 'servant' was the term used for anybody who worked on a nobleman's estate, no matter what their specific job might be.) Tempers finally boiled over in 1461, when the two families engaged in a War of the Roses in miniature within the Bashall Eaves district. In this year the Singletons attacked Bashall Hall with a force of over 100 men. The Talbots would certainly not forgive or forget this assault on their home, which must have led to substantial casualties. The Talbots and their allies licked their wounds and bided their time, waiting for an opportunity to exact revenge on their hated neighbours.

In 1465, Sir Thomas Talbot was the prime mover in a famous incident which was to guarantee his family a place in the annals of English history. Sir Thomas and his sons had discovered that the Lancastrian king Henry VI was hiding out at Waddington, only a few miles from Bashall Hall. If the Talbot family could contrive to capture the hapless King Henry and hand him over to his Yorkist rival, royal favour from Edward IV would be assured. The Talbot wealth and status would receive a tremendous boost. It was far too good an opportunity to miss.

After his defeat at Hexham in May 1464, King Henry had fled south, and taken refuge with supporters in the Clitheroe area. He had with him a couple of companions, Dr. John Bedon, a clerk of Oxford and Dr. Thomas Mannynge, the former Dean of Windsor along

The headless statue of Peg o' Nell presiding over her well on the banks of the River Ribble at Waddow Hall, Brungerley, near Clitheroe.

The statue is that of a saint, which in all likelihood was beheaded by Protestants during the sixteenth or seventeenth centuries. It probably stood originally in a private chapel within the manor house. This was owned by the Tempests, one of the leading Roman Catholic families of the area.
Photo: author

The so-called boot, glove and spoon of Henry VI, said to have been left by the king at Bolton Hall, Bolton-by-Bowland, where he had sought refuge prior to his stay at Waddington Hall. Upon examination these personal items were found to date from the seventeenth century rather than the fifteenth and were not, therefore, genuine relics of St. Henry.
Whittaker's History and Antiquities of Craven

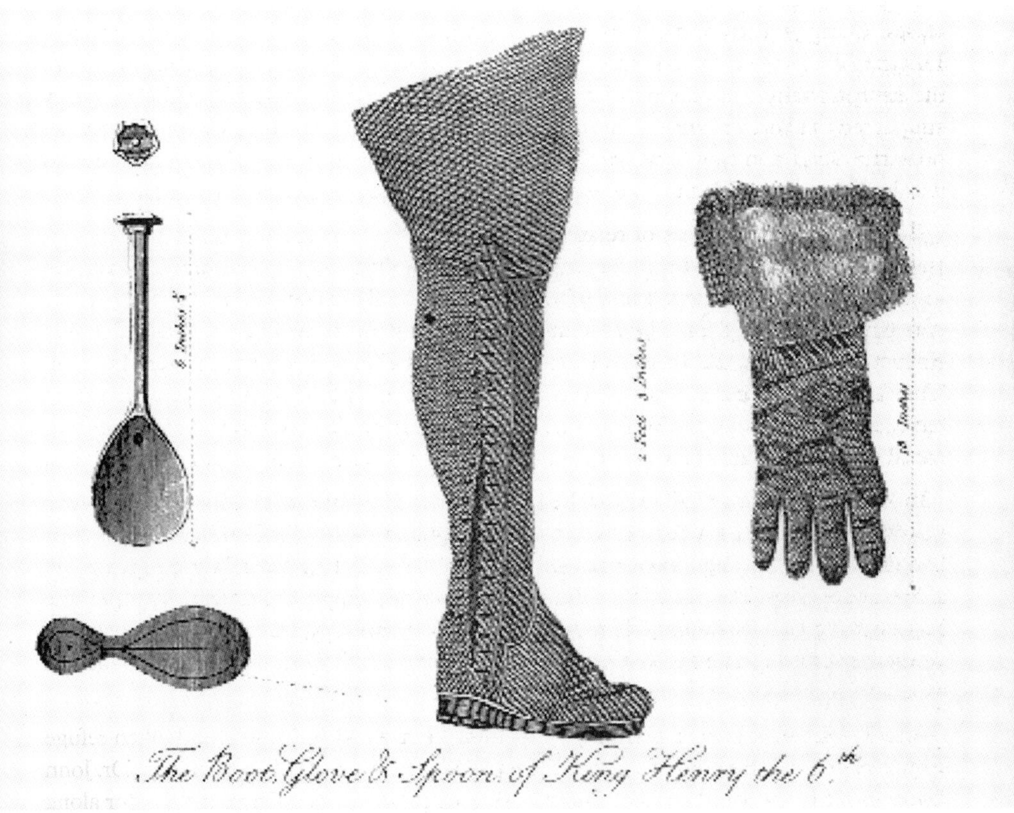

with a young man called Ellerton. Initially the fugitives stayed with Sir Ralph Pudsey at Bolton Hall, but later sought refuge at Waddington Hall, a property belonging to Sir John Tempest. This was a bad move, as Sir Thomas Talbot of Bashall Hall was married to Alice Tempest, Sir John's daughter, and it was only a matter of time before word reached the Talbot family of the royal fugitive hiding out nearby.

Henry was feeling far from secure at Waddington Hall in any case, it would seem. It is recorded in The Memoir of John Blacman that he had a premonition that he was about to be betrayed. *"As he lay hid there for some time, an audible voice sounded in his ears for some 17 days before he was taken, telling him how he would be delivered up by treachery....And when he told this to Masters Bedon and Mannynge, they were incredulous and believed it not, but thought it all to be but vain wanderings until the event assured them of the truth."*

An interesting (if somewhat confusing) account of the capture of Henry VI appears in John Warkworth's Chronicle, an early source certainly written by 1483 and thus within 20 years of the events it was describing. Its detail suggests that the author had the benefit of local knowledge, possibly gained from an eye-witness account of the events in question.

"Also the same yere, Kynge Herry was takene bysyde a howse of religione in Lancaschyre, by the mene of a blacke monke of Abyngtone, in a wode called Cletherwode, besyde Bungerly Hyppnyngstones, by Thomas Talbot, sonne and heyre to Sere Edmunde Talbot of Basshalle, and Jhon Talbot his cosyne of Colebry, with other moo; whiche disseyvide, beyngne at his dynere at Wadyngtone Halle, and caryed to Londone on horse bake, and his lege bownde to the styrope and so brought thrugh London to the Toure."

What seems to have happened is this. Having ascertained Henry's presence at Waddington Old Hall, Sir Thomas Talbot of Bashall, his cousin John Talbot of Salesbury (Colebry) and others arrived at the hall just as King Henry was sitting down to a meal. The king somehow managed to evade them (local tradition says he escaped by means of a secret stair) and ran off with his companions across the fields towards Clitheroe. The king got as far as the River Ribble, which marked the boundary between Yorkshire and Lancashire. He crossed the river into Lancashire at Brungerley by means of the Hipping (or Hippin) Stones. These were large stepping stones, about 55 in all, set at an acute angle across the river and a few yards upstream from the present bridge. (A particularly dry spell in 1992 enabled the exploration of the dried-up river bed. It was established that, regrettably, no original Hipping Stones remain in situ.)

Henry could not evade his pursuers indefinitely and he was eventually captured, we are told, beside a house of religion close to the Hipping Stones. This 'house of religion' was in all probability a hermitage, established at the dangerous river crossing so that a resident hermit (or group of hermits) might assist travellers across the stepping stones.* The crossing at Brungerley was a famously treacherous one, resulting in many fatalities

---

* A hermit named William Marshall was licensed to celebrate mass in the Chapel of St. Oswald at Waddington Church in 1444. The location of his hermitage is unknown, but may have been at Brungerley.

by drowning, until the present bridge was erected in 1816. The notorious reputation of the Hipping Stones over the centuries has even resulted in the growth of a local legend. This tells of Peg O' Nell, a local water spirit, (some say ghost) who claims sacrifice here on "Peg's Night" every seven years*. Brungerley, then, was a prime site for the foundation of a hermitage site, where Henry may have sought shelter after he had crossed the Ribble.

The role played by the black monk of Abyngtone, who was also instrumental in the capture of Henry, is rather a mystery. Other sources name him as William Cantlowe. He may have been a member of the Benedictine Order, whose monks wore black habits, or he may have been a member of the Black Canons. Where he hailed from is as uncertain as the monastic order to which he belonged. Abyngtone might possibly be Abingdon in Oxfordshire, as other writers have suggested. A Benedictine Monastery certainly existed here, but there is a difficulty in that the name of this town never took the form Abyngtone in medieval times. An intriguing possibility is that the black monk may have been one of the serving brothers resident at Brungerley hermitage, but without further evidence this must, for the moment, remain pure speculation.

The wood (Cletherwode) in which Henry was captured appears to be the four acres or so of woodland whose later name was Christian Pightle (meaning a small, irregular piece of land), which was probably more extensive in the fifteenth century. This land was situated close to the Hipping Stones on the Clitheroe side of the river.

When the Talbots finally caught up with their quarry in Clitheroe Wood, Henry was placed upon a horse with his feet tied to the stirrups. Powerless though he might have seemed to his foes, Henry nevertheless swiftly managed to wipe the smiles off the faces of Sir Thomas Talbot and his cronies. For, as he left on the long journey which would end at the Tower of London, Henry placed a perpetual curse upon the Talbots of Bashall Hall.

The Curse of King Henry VI

Henry's curse is said to have taken the form of a prediction that there would be nine generations of Talbots consisting of a wise man and a fool, by turns, and then the family name would cease to exist. The curse in this particular form was not recorded until the mid-seventeenth century, by Christopher Townley, and it is possible that its content and wording became somewhat diluted and sanitised over the years. A malediction of any kind placed upon a family was taken very seriously indeed in those superstitious days, and Henry's words doubtless chilled Sir Thomas Talbot to the bone.

However, he managed to put it to the back of his mind for the time being, and enjoyed the fruits of his labours. The grateful Yorkist king, Edward IV, rewarded Sir Thomas well for the capture of his great rival. As well as awarding him a lump sum of 100 shillings in cash, Edward also remitted the annual rent of £8-10s-7d for the manor of Bashall and

---

*The next "Peg's Night" is due at Christmas time, 2006

granted Thomas a yearly pension of 40 shillings. In the following year, Sir Thomas's sons, Edmund, William and Thomas also received a cash reward for assisting their father in his efforts. Interestingly, Sir John Tempest, the owner of Waddington Hall, also received a reward from Edward IV. This suggests that there was far more to the affair than met the eye, and that King Henry VI had every reason to feel insecure while under Sir John's 'protection'.

As the leaders of the endeavour, the Talbot family emerged from the affair in triumph. Their power and influence in the area could no longer be challenged. Revenge is always a dish best served cold, and with this in mind, the eyes of the Talbots fell stonily upon their hated enemies the Singletons of Withgill. In 1469 the Talbots finally settled their scores with this family. Their vengeance took the particularly nasty form of a brutal murder of a female member of the Singleton clan. The Coroner's Inquest records that:

"John Talbot, son of Margaret Talbot of Bashall, gentleman, on 12th January 1469, at Mitton, of great malice long thought out, struck the said Alice [Singleton] in the breast with a lance, price sixpence, and gave her a mortal blow and she instantly died."

So that was the end of Alice Singleton it would seem. Not quite, for a small queue appears to have formed behind John Talbot.

"And Richard Talbot of Bashall, gentleman, struck her with an arrow and gave her a mortal blow in the lower part of the head, as far as the brain: and Thrustan Waddington, of Syghton, co. York, yoman, struck her with a stick called a longdebeve on the right side of her belly which would have killed her but that she was already dead."

Thomas Talbot of Bashall, Nicholas Tempest of Bracewell and scores of other Talbot relatives and supporters were present, and aided and abetted this premeditated murder. What Alice Singleton had personally done (if anything) to warrant such vicious treatment is unclear, but it didn't really matter because the members of the murder squad were given the King's Pardon as they were all loyal Yorkists! It would appear that nobody had heard of the Age of Chivalry in these wild northern realms, and it seems that justice was also in rather short supply.

All powerful and secure the Talbots might then have felt within their own manors, but as he got older, it seems that Sir Thomas's mind began to be haunted by the memory of King Henry's curse. Since his death in 1471 Henry VI had widely come to be regarded as a saint, and a cult of St. Henry sprang up accordingly. Henry was never officially canonised, but his cult certainly existed not only in Windsor but in the Talbot's 'own back yard', so to speak, at Whalley Abbey. The earliest written record of an offering at the altar of King Henry at Whalley is in 1510.

It is more than probable, therefore, that the Talbots found themselves progressively more unpopular in the Clitheroe area, as the perpetrators of an act of betrayal. To betray an anointed king was bad enough. But as Henry gradually transformed into a saint the Talbots' actions took on a whole new significance and were doubtless regarded as increasingly obnoxious. The idea of his curse now became supernaturally terrifying to any good Catholic. Apprehensive, therefore, that the saintly king's curse would prove effective and result in his illustrious name dying out, Sir Thomas finally decided to take pre-emptive action to avert the prospect.

In 1498, two years before he died, Sir Thomas Talbot made a deed of perpetuity by which he entrusted the management of all his manors to Thomas Tempest, Thomas Ashton and others. Sir Thomas himself stated that the purpose of this deed was so that his estates *"may remain in the heirs males of my body lawfully begotten, and in the name of the Talbots for ever."* He instructed that a copy of the deed should be brought to Whalley Abbey after he died *"there to remaine for evermore"*.

Shortly after the death of Sir Thomas in 1500, the Talbots appear to have rented out Bashall Hall to tenants, residing instead for the most part at Audley Hall in Blackburn. One of the tenants of Bashall Hall whose name has come down to us is Nicholas Tempest, the younger brother of Sir Richard Tempest of Bracewell. In 1536 Nicholas became embroiled in the religious rebellion against King Henry VIII known as The Pilgrimage of Grace. Robert Aske, one of the leaders of the revolt, came with 300 followers to Monubent, nine miles north-east of Bashall, where Nicholas was pressed into service as a recruiting officer. He was sent to Whalley Abbey to pressurise John Paslew, the last abbot of Whalley, into joining the endeavour.

Henry VIII put down the rebellion with his usual ruthless efficiency and made examples of the northern Catholic rebels. Nicholas Tempest thus found himself a prisoner in the Tower of London. He was condemned to death, along with Robert Aske and several others, on May 9th 1537. On Friday, 25th May, Nicholas was tied on his back to a hurdle and dragged through the London streets to Tyburn, where he suffered the appalling ordeal of execution by hanging, drawing and quartering. Living at the old Talbot manor house as a tenant had certainly brought Nicholas Tempest no luck whatsoever.

By the beginning of the seventeenth century it became clear that all Sir Thomas Talbot's attempts to avert the effects of the curse had failed. The last Talbot of Bashall was Thomas, whose parents John Talbot and Ursula Hamerton were immortalised in portraits painted on boards once to be found at Hellifield Peel. In his History of Whalley, Whittaker has this to say about the portraits:

"John Talbot is represented as a large, stern, bluff-looking man; but I have heard a very good judge of painting and physiognomy observe, that the boy has the features of an idiot. The lady does not seem to have been likely, from the expression of her countenance, to redeem the Talbots from that failure of intellect to which they are reported to have been subject every second generation. These portraits . . . though very indifferently painted, cannot but afford some pleasure to an antiquary, as the only existing remains of that ancient family."

Unfortunately all attempts to track down the present whereabouts of these paintings have failed. Thomas Talbot, John and Ursula's son, died in 1619 without having produced a surviving male heir to carry on his illustrious name. Henry VI's curse had come to fruition even earlier than he had predicted. The Talbot name was extinct.

No likenesses of family members can now be traced, and even their final resting places are a mystery.* Only the Talbot manor house remained, already haunted by its violent past, with Henry's curse lingering in the air.

After the Talbots

After the death of the last male Talbot, Bashall Hall was inherited by his daughters, one of whom married Colonel William White. Bashall Hall passed out of the family entirely when Thomas Talbot's daughter died, and Colonel White subsequently remarried. It is unlikely that Colonel White ever paid more than fleeting visits to Bashall Hall, as his principal residence was elsewhere and it is said that the house went to rack and ruin during the Civil War. Future owners of the hall included the Ferrers family who lived there from 1678-1707, and spent much time and effort on the garden but apparently very little on the house itself.

By 1767 Hugh Lloyd had inherited Bashall Hall. At this time, or very shortly afterwards, it seems that the hall was again let out to tenants as the Country Notebook of Thomas Oakes of Harrop Hall contains the following entry for 1802: *"Bashall Hall Etc. Mr. Lloyd's Estate Letts for £800 per annum - for which he has refused from Mr Fielding £32,000."*

Mr Lloyd's tenants were in all probability members of the Dawson family, who would continue to live at Bashall Hall and farm the estate for the next couple of centuries or so. The Dawsons had already lived in the area for many years. The first mention of a Dawson in the village of Worston is in 1376. Thereafter members of the family regularly served as Halmote jurors in Worston and Chatburn in medieval times, often holding the office of Greave, Constable and Churchwarden. The first member of the family to live at Bashall Hall as tenant farmer was James Dawson, the great-great-grandfather of the James Dawson whose life and unsolved murder in 1934 is our main concern. Jim's great-great-grandfather was born in Pendleton and died at Bashall Hall in 1797. In 1806 Bashall Hall was sold to the Taylor (later Worsley-Taylor) family, in whose ownership it remained until the estate was sold to the Barnes family in 1972.

In his "Buildings of England" (1969), art historian Nikolaus Pevsner described Bashall Hall as *"an uncommonly interesting and impressive house. It consists of parts of various dates and is surrounded by walled gardens and accessory buildings."* Most manor houses developed organically over the years, with each successive owner demolishing, adding to and adapting the original building according to the dictates of fashion and purse.

Any medieval manor house required a handy water supply. Bashall Hall stands on the banks of Bashall Brook, which some people identify with the River Bassas where King Arthur fought a battle against the Saxons. In summer, this rippling stream presents an

---

* No memorial to a medieval member of the Talbot family of Bashall Hall, including the notorious Sir Thomas, has ever been recorded at Mitton Church.

idyllic picture of tranquillity. In winter, however, it can quickly transform into a dangerous and swift-flowing torrent.

Earthworks representing medieval fish ponds have been identified close to the present hall, and may represent a survival from the earlier house. These supplied the Talbot family with fresh fish such as eel, perch, roach and tench, and were a common feature of many medieval manor houses

The original medieval hall was probably remodelled or rebuilt from scratch in the mid-fifteenth century, a period during which many manor houses underwent improvement and when the Talbot star was in the ascendant. The spirit of Sir Thomas Talbot would have great difficulty orientating itself in Bashall Hall today. However, there is one building which he would probably recognise instantaneously, as in all likelihood it has changed very little since his day. This is the building known as 'The Barracks' located to the rear of the house. The Royal Commission on the Historical Monuments of England describes the barracks as a two-storey building, the upper part of which is constructed of timber-framing with wattle and daub infill. 80 feet long by 25 feet wide, it has a number of small and apparently unheated rooms connected by an open gallery.

Tradition states that it was here that the Talbot family housed their 'private army'. This private army, if it can be called such, basically consisted of the Talbots' servants, and the servants of their noble friends and allies in the district. These servants would, of course, have been expected to fight for their liege lord at a moment's notice, and might well have worn the Talbot livery at times, but most of their time would have been spent working on the land. It is unlikely, therefore, that the building known as The Barracks was used exclusively as soldiers' quarters, although the building may well have been utilised for this purpose on more than one occasion.

By Tudor times Bashall Hall itself had five gables, three in the centre and one at each end. A private chapel occupied the whole of the upper storey. At some point the east wing was demolished and the whole building lowered by removing the top storey.

It was at this beautiful old manor house, over which lingered the curse of a saintly king and the violent deeds of those who captured him, that Jim Dawson was born and lived out his eventful and tragic life.

CHAPTER 2

The Dawsons of Bashall Hall

BORN on June 3rd 1887, Jim Dawson was the fifth child of Matthew and Mary Dawson, two cousins from the neighbouring farms of Bashall Hall and Cheetall. In this small and relatively static rural community, the marriage of cousins was a fairly common occurrence in those days.

Matthew Dawson, Jim's father, ran the Bashall Hall estate in partnership with his younger brother Charles. On her marriage to Matthew in 1876, when she was 23 years old, Mary Dawson left the seventeenth-century farmhouse of Cheetall to join her husband and his bachelor brother at Bashall.

Matthew and Mary's close family relationship did not in any way hamper their enthusiasm for procreation. In the nineteen years of their marriage, Mary presented her cousin Matthew with an impressive brood of twelve children. The eldest, Polly*, was born in 1876. Tragedy struck the family early when William, born two years later, drowned in Bashall Brook when only a year old in 1879. The circumstances surrounding the accident are unclear. It has been said, however, that his mother Mary was severely censured by the Coroner at the Inquest, as she had been absent from home shopping in Clitheroe at the time of the accident.

In the same year that William perished in Bashall Brook, Mary gave birth to a son whom she named John.** After a break of three years, Mary and Matthew celebrated the birth of another son. They christened this fourth baby William. It seems peculiar to bestow upon this baby the same name as his drowned brother. Possibly his parents intended it to be a tribute to his memory but I would personally have considered the name ill-fated and avoided its use a second time.

My grandmother Lily† was born in 1884, followed by Jim himself in 1887 and Harry in 1888. Annie was born in 1889 and Felix two years later. In 1892 baby Bob came along. By this time Jim's mother finally seems to have got herself some domestic assistance. The Census return for 1891 mentions a Mary Wake and Sarah Anne Wake (presumably sisters) as servants residing at Bashall Hall. The household at this time comprised fifteen people including two male servants who assisted Matthew and Charles in the running of the farm estate.

---

* She was actually christened Mary, but was always known as Polly.
** John was always known as Jack, but for clarity we will refer to him as John throughout.
† Lily was actually christened Elizabeth Hannah

As a middle child Jim Dawson cannot have received much parental care or affection as he was growing up. Indeed in those days farmers' children received very little personal attention at the best of times and appeared to have been left to their own devices on a regular basis. This is not entirely surprising with families being so large and the constant housework and farm to worry about.

Jim commenced his education at Bashall Eaves village school when he was six years old on 23rd April, 1893. Two weeks later an older boy called Tommy Simpson arrived at the school. Tommy was eleven years old and living at nearby Hodder House at the time. We will hear a lot more about Tommy, who knew Jim Dawson all his life. Both men died under extremely unusual circumstances, Jim by the hand of a murderer in 1934 and Tommy by his own hand a couple of years later. In 1896 another of Jim's lifelong friends was admitted to the school. Bill Eccles remembers Jim as *'nobbut an ordinary school lad'*, who was very quiet and not particularly interested in sport or anything else for that matter. It is difficult to envisage many scintillating conversations ever having taken place between these two young men.

Mary and Matthew Dawson produced two final daughters after Jim had started school. His sister Margaret was born in 1894 and last but not least, Greta arrived on the scene in 1895. The family was now complete. There is no reason to suppose that Mary had any medical assistance whatsoever in the birthing of her twelve children. While Polly, as eldest daughter, would doubtless have lent a hand at the births of her younger siblings, it did not seem to be the custom to engage a professional midwife.

Another Bashall Eaves lady who produced numerous children dealt with everything entirely on her own. I am told that when she felt a baby about to be born, she sent the rest of her children outside, got into bed, gave birth, got up again, cleaned up the mess and then cooked dinner. This no-nonsense approach seems almost beyond belief today. My personal response to childbirth was, *"Give me drugs. Give me some drugs. An epidural. Gas. Any drugs. NOW!"*

The strain of producing so many children inevitably took its toll on the health of Jim's mother. Mary Dawson died of a throat tumour on May 3rd in 1895 at the age of 42. Exhaustion must surely have contributed to her death. Two years later Jim also lost his father. Matthew Dawson died horribly of blood poisoning in the head as a result of contracting anthrax. Anthrax is one of the oldest and deadliest diseases known to man. Known also as 'Black Bane' and 'The Fifth Plague' it was an occupational hazard of working with livestock. Matthew contracted the disease while shearing sheep. The infection penetrated his exposed skin, causing itchy spots on his head which then blistered and turned into relatively painless ulcers with a black base. The infection subsequently spread to his bloodstream which caused septicaemia and circulatory collapse. In the absence of antibiotics, Matthew had practically no chance of survival and he died on May 15th 1897.

Thus was Jim Dawson orphaned at the age of ten. Later that same year, misfortune again befell the family, for on December 5th Jim's little sister Margaret also died.

Jim Dawson's Family

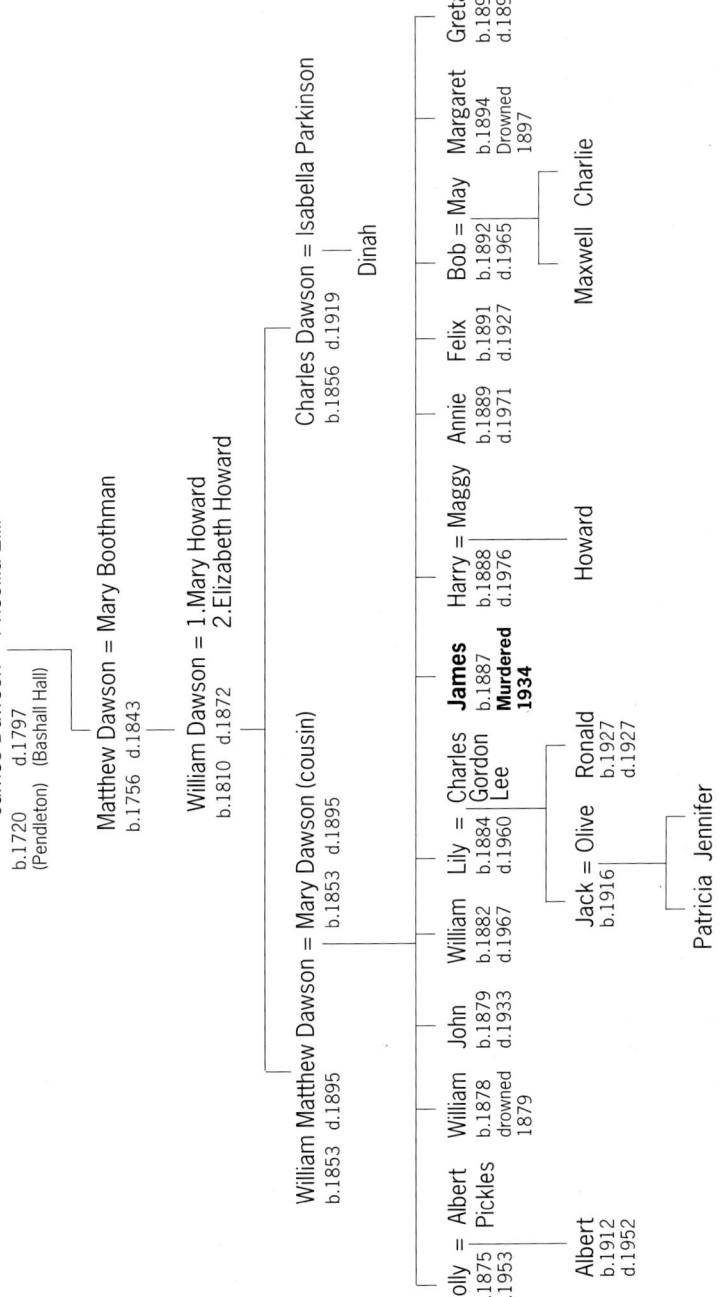

The Dawson family in front of Bashall Hall circa 1880. On the far left is Jim's Uncle Charles. Standing next to Charles is his cousin Hannah. Seated in the middle is John Dawson (formerly of Cheetall Farm) a fearsome patriarch who used to brandish a stick. In front of him stands an understandably morose-looking little Polly Dawson. To the right stand her (and Jim's) parents, the cousins William Matthew Dawson and Mary Dawson. *Photo: family archive*

Three-year-old Margaret somehow drowned in the horse trough which at that time was situated close to the main door of Bashall Hall. (It has since been moved near to The Barracks.)

The local water spirits seemed determined to victimise the Dawson children, or perhaps the Dawson family of Bashall Hall were now coming under the influence of the curse of Henry VI, but in a more deadly and malignant form. Certainly the family seemed to be suffering more than its fair share of tragedy.

Upon the death of his older brother Matthew, Charles Dawson had become head of the Bashall Hall household. Jim Dawson's Uncle Charles was at this time a 38 year old bachelor and his attitude towards sharing the hall with his brother's ten orphaned children is not recorded. It may be deduced, perhaps, from the fact that a year after the death of his father, Jim's brother Harry was sent away from Bashall Hall to earn his living on a neighbouring farm. Harry was ten years old at the time.

By 1898, Lily Dawson appears to have left home to take up residence at Colliers, another Dawson farm on the hill known as The Nab, near Whalley. Possibly she was needed there to nurse her sister Greta, who died of a diseased hip at Colliers in this particular year. By 1901 William had gone into service at a nearby farm called Micklehurst. The adult members of the household at Bashall Hall were thus reduced to Charles Dawson, Polly and John. Jim, along with Annie, Felix and Bob, was still attending Bashall Eaves School.

Bashall Eaves Day School, attended by Jim Dawson and his family and friends. Some of the schoolbooks of Matthew Dawson, Jim's father, are used as a local history resource for present day schoolchildren at Clitheroe Library.
Photo: author

An almost unbelievably neat example of work from Matthew Dawson's mathematics book carried out when he was only 10 years old in 1863.
Family archive

Charles takes a Wife

Change was in the air for Jim and his brothers and sisters, for at the late age of 47, their Uncle Charles finally took himself a wife. His bride Isabella was 37 years old. It is said that Charles had managed to impregnate two women at the same time, which was careless of him. Whatever the truth of the matter, it was Isabella whom he chose to make his bride. What became of the other lady and her illegitimate offspring is unknown. In May of the following year, Charles and Isabella were blessed by the birth of a daughter whom they named Dinah.

Shortly after Charles and Isabella started their family, the formal partnership between Charles and his late brother Matthew's family was abruptly dissolved. Charles had probably decided that now he was married with a family of his own, he and Isabella had no further use for his brother's orphaned children cluttering up the place. The potential for family quarrels was infinite and it may well have been as a result of such a quarrel that Matthew's children departed. Charles Dawson was not, by all accounts, an easy man to get on with, being partial to a drink or fifty.

In contrast to Charles, the Dawson women were widely perceived as being rather prim and proper young ladies. This is illustrated by one particular occasion when Annie and Lily Dawson were taking the air at Back Commons in Clitheroe. Spotting the two elegant young ladies from a distance, two local lads decided to follow them and try their luck. When they were close enough to recognise their quarry, the boys quickly realised their mistake. In great disappointment they exclaimed, *"Oh, it's Annie and Lily Dawson. Nowt doing there!"* and sloped off.

Polly, John and the rest of the family (with one exception) left Bashall Hall in 1903 and removed to Colliers Farm in Billington. Only one of Matthew's children chose to remain at the hall and that was Jim Dawson, now aged 16.

Jim Learns Farming

In 1934 Isabella Dawson described Jim's status at Bashall Hall at this time as 'servant' to her husband Charles. To describe a nephew as a servant might sound a little odd to modern ears. A farm servant was generally an adolescent boy who was hired for one year at a time and who lived on the farm as a member of the family. (A farm labourer, conversely, was usually a married man who lived elsewhere and who was paid a daily or weekly wage.) Boys taken on as farm servants would attend the local hiring fair (presumably not necessary in Jim's case), where they were contracted at an agreed wage, with their board and lodging thrown in.

Farm service had been a common career choice for many young boys since medieval times. After the mid-eighteenth century it subsequently declined in the south of England as farmers ceased to treat the young male servants as members of the family. In other parts of the country, Bashall Eaves evidently being one of them, the arrangement survived through the nineteenth century and well into the twentieth. The term 'servant' has an almost feudal ring to it by this late stage in its history.

It is probable, therefore, that Jim was treated no differently from any other servant at Bashall Hall, being an orphan and in need of earning his keep. We do not really know what sort of relationship he had with his uncle Charles and it is interesting to speculate what sort of influence Charles may have had in the formation of Jim's character and attitudes when he was at such an impressionable age. Presumably Jim did not particularly dislike his uncle or he would not have chosen to remain within his household.

Jim Dawson was not, of course, the only servant employed by Charles and Isabella. In 1903 a female servant at Bashall Hall provided a bit of local excitement when her antics resulted in a police enquiry and court hearing. The Clitheroe Advertiser and Times reported the strange case on 27th November, 1903.

Jim's uncle, Charles Dawson, circa 1880. Jim Dawson worked as his Uncle Charles' farm servant at Bashall Hall from 1903 until 1909.
Photo: family archive

The Spiteful Servant

Isabella Dawson had engaged the services of a woman called Edith Vyner as a domestic servant in August, presumably to replace Polly Dawson who was no longer available to act as the family dogsbody.

On Saturday 14th November, Isabella went into her bedroom and wound up her silver watch, which was worth £3. She placed it on the mantelshelf and returned downstairs to find that Charles and his two servants (one of whom was Jim) had arrived to have tea together.

According to Isabella, after the men had gone outside again, Edith Vyner went upstairs, came back down again and then went outside to collect some firewood from the stack near Bashall Brook. When Edith returned, Isabella said that she herself left the house for about fifteen minutes to feed some calves, leaving Edith the only person present in the house (apart, presumably, from her baby daughter Dinah).

When Isabella returned from tending the animals, she discovered the front door wide open and was startled to see that one of her husband's vests had been tossed outside. On entering the house, she saw that his best clothes had been strewn around the floor. One of Jim's vests was also subsequently found to be missing.

Isabella confronted Edith as the only adult person in the house, saying that somebody must have broken in.

Edith replied, *"I heard a noise but I thought it was the cat."* (A likely story.)

Having by now realised that her watch was missing from the bedroom, Isabella called the police and P.C. Surr arrived to try to solve the exciting vest mystery. It wasn't long before the eager policeman spotted one of the vests floating in full view in Bashall Brook. He arrested Edith Vyner and charged her on suspicion of stealing the watch and a vest containing three shillings. Edith moaned, *"I have not got it and you cannot lock me up if I have not got the watch."*

After a week or so of prowling round the farm, Isabella eventually gazed into the depths of Bashall Brook near the wood stack and spotted her watch there. (You would have thought that this was the first place anybody would look!) Edith Vyner was then charged but persisted with her dodgy defence. *"I did not steal them. I simply threw them away."* She was later committed for one month without hard labour at Bolton Sessions on 23rd November. What a silly servant.

Nevertheless this is a bizarre little episode and there may have been more to it than met the eye. Reading between the lines it seems likely that Charles, Jim or Isabella (or all of them) had upset this servant in some way, leading to this spiteful incident. Either that or Edith Vyner was, to put it politely, a bit simple and one of the most inept thieves in the history of crime. Be that as it may, this tale provides yet another peculiar episode in the annals of Bashall Hall history.

The bridge over Bashall Brook (taken circa 1980), in which Jim Dawson's brother William drowned in 1879. In the background can be seen The Barracks with a glimpse of Bashall Hall behind this building.
Photo: N. J. Cobban

During these years as one of his Uncle Charles' servants, Jim Dawson would learn everything there was to know about the running of a dairy farm estate, by hands-on experience. Having lived on the farm all his life, he would already have acquired some expertise and a great deal of general knowledge about the care of stock. Jim's career as a farmer had always been mapped out for him and we have to wonder if other options ever even occurred to him.

In 1905 a group of ramblers led by a man called J.T. Fielding gained permission from the Worsley-Taylor family to look around Bashall Hall, which cannot have pleased its residents much. Fielding's report of the visit provides an interesting snapshot of Jim Dawson's home at that time. Even then, Fielding says, the hall was *'crumbling under the severe grip of Father Time'*. The ancient gateway to the house had been walled up because the Dawsons were annoyed at the number of sightseers who came to peep. In those days, *"the remains of a fine avenue of trees down which the Lords of Bashall rode in splendour in the days of Henry VI could still be seen"*. Inside the hall itself, *"The rooms are surrounded by oak panelling in good state of preservation, though some white paint recently smeared upon it, has not enhanced its appearance at all."*

Thoroughly unimpressed with the Dawson family's attempts at interior décor (and who can blame them) Fielding then went on to describe the rooms on the first floor of the hall as having once been covered with tapestries. By 1905 these had apparently disappeared apart from two pieces. Faded and crumbling, they were scarcely decipherable.

It is, of course, a great pity that so much of the historic fabric of Bashall Hall was allowed to disintegrate over the years through neglect and ignorance. However we should bear in mind that the old hall was also a working farmhouse, and as tenants the Dawson family had neither the time nor the money to indulge in conservation projects.*

Colliers, Backridge and the Great War

Jim Dawson remained in the service of his Uncle Charles amid the faded grandeur of Bashall Hall for six years. In 1909, when he was 22 years old, Jim decided to join the rest of his family at Colliers Farm at Billington. We do not know what prompted this decision but it may be that he felt he had learned as much as he could from Charles and it was time to move on.

It must have been a pleasant change for Jim to be able to work alongside his big brother John and to have his sisters Polly, Lily and Annie to look after him once more. His elder sister Polly had been working as the manageress of Colne Dairy, but in 1910 she contracted a septic hand and returned to the family at Colliers. Polly did not stay put for long, however. For in 1912 she married a widowed farmer called Albert Pickles and

---

*This was a cause of much regret to the Dawson family – particularly to Polly Pickles, who was intensely proud of the old building.

moved to his farm "Gincroft" at Edenfield, near Manchester. She gave birth to her first and only child on 24th April 1912 and the baby boy was named Albert after his father. Tragedy then struck its inevitable blow when Polly's husband died only nine months after the wedding, leaving her to look after a new baby and run her husband's farm single-handedly. Fortune never seemed to smile on Polly Pickles for long.

In 1913 everything changed yet again for Jim Dawson and his family. John and Jim (with their younger brother Harry) made the decision to leave Colliers and go into partnership together at the beautiful mid-eighteenth century farm at Backridge in Bashall Eaves. During gravel digging in the early nineteenth century, many skeletons were discovered near this farmhouse, along with broken bronze-age axes and brooches. Some have speculated that these bones represent casualties of a battle fought in the vicinity. It is unlikely, however, that valuable re-usable bronzes would be abandoned. The gravel diggers probably disturbed bronze-age burial mounds, the bronze items having been broken symbolically to send them into the next world along with their owners.

On the outbreak of the Great War in 1914, Polly Pickles resolved to rent out her farm at Edenfield and move to Backridge. Her decision was without a doubt prompted by the fact that she had recently undergone major surgery for breast cancer. It is therefore understandable that she wished to have her close family around her at this time of personal and national crisis.

Jim Dawson was 27 when the Great War started. In common with the majority of young men at the time he was, no doubt, eager to do his bit for England by enlisting to serve in the army. However, farmers were needed on the land and for the time being it seems that Jim stayed put at Backridge, probably intending to join up should it prove necessary. The farmers did their best to contribute to the war effort in other ways. In October, 1914, for example, Bashall Eaves offered its full support to The Belgian Relief Fund in aid of distressed families in Belgium. Charles Dawson of Bashall Hall donated 10 shillings, while the Dawson brothers of Backridge contributed 5 shillings to the fund.

A couple of months earlier Jim's brother, John Dawson, had received rather a shock. While tending the cows, John happened to look up and was horrified to see 'a giant German Zeppelin' cruising low over Bashall Hall and heading towards Backridge. He was apparently (and not surprisingly) so terrified that he dived under the nearest hedge to escape the airship's notice. John was not the only person to witness this alarming sight. The Clitheroe Advertiser and Times reported on August 28th 1914 that, *"It is confidently stated by a number of men who are perforce spending their nights out of doors that during the week an airship has been seen manoeuvring in the locality."*

Jim Dawson was still in England on May 4th 1915 for on that date Jim and Annie were witnesses at the marriage of their sister Lily to Charles Gordon Lee at All Hallows Church at Mitton. Lily had met Charles while he was learning farming at Bashall Town. Lily's husband enlisted in November 1914 and served in the Middle East as a machine gunner with the Cheshire Regiment.

Jim Dawson proudly showing off his army uniform in 1916. This is the only known photograph of the murder victim. *Photo: family archive*

Jim himself appears to have enlisted in the army some time in 1916, but details of his life during this period are particularly scanty. From an examination of a family photograph of Jim in army uniform, it has been possible to conclude that he joined the Lincolnshire Regiment. Why he did not join the local East Lancashire Regiment is unclear, but it is interesting to note that his brother Bob had joined the Bedfordshire Regiment back in 1914. Presumably, therefore, volunteers were placed in regiments which were under strength. Family tradition states that Jim acted as a stretcher-bearer during the war, and that he was wounded in action.

Jim appears as a 'Living Ghost'

One of Annie Dawson's favourite stories about her brother Jim takes us into the realms of the supernatural. According to Annie, the family had received a telegram during the war containing the bad news that he had gone missing in action. Some time later, Annie was asleep in bed in the middle of the night and suddenly awoke, feeling a presence in the room. To her astonishment she saw Jim's figure standing at the foot of her bed looking down at her. *"Don't worry, Annie, I'm alright,"* he said to her and then promptly vanished. Although startled, Annie was not in the least frightened by the experience. Shortly afterwards, the family rejoiced at the welcome news that Jim had been found.

This particular sort of spectral appearance is known as a 'ghost of the living', or a "crisis apparition" and is a relatively well-known if puzzling phenomenon in the annals of psychical research. In these cases a person, under particular conditions not yet understood, is seen in one place when they are somewhere else entirely. Jim's appearance to Annie might also be explained by the phenomenon known as 'astral projection', where the spirit or essence of a person travels to another place in visible form while the physical body remains paralysed in another location. This is said to happen spontaneously at times of physical or mental crisis (although it can be learned). It is possible, therefore, that Jim was in the throes of a life-threatening emergency at the time of his appearance to Annie who was far away in England. (It is, of course, equally possible that Annie was dreaming though she always denied this vehemently.)

Annie Dawson, Jim's sister, circa 1914.
Photo: family archive

Return to Bashall Hall

As the soldiers wended their weary way home from the various fronts, Charles Dawson's health was deteriorating. On February 8th 1919 he died at Bashall Hall and was interred in the graveyard at Mitton Church. Within seven weeks his widow Isabella and her daughter Dinah had left the hall and moved to Pimlico Road in Clitheroe. Jim Dawson and his brother Bob had by this time returned to England and Charles Gordon Lee had also returned home safely to Jim's sister Lily. For the first time, Charles Gordon saw his son Jack, who had been born at Backridge three years earlier.

As Bashall Hall was now lying vacant, John, Jim and Harry Dawson dissolved their partnership at Backridge Farm. No doubt with a degree of grim satisfaction, John and Jim moved back to Bashall Hall, taking with them Polly as their housekeeper. Harry remained at Backridge, keeping sister Annie with him to act as his housekeeper.

The future must now have looked bright to the Dawson family. The war was over and Matthew Dawson's sons had regained what they doubtless considered their rightful position at Bashall Hall. An atmosphere of optimism enveloped the whole of Bashall Eaves as its residents looked forward to the peace celebrations. These took place on September 11th 1919 and consisted of musical entertainments, feasting and sporting activities held on the field in front of the Red Pump Hotel. Miss Worsley-Taylor handed to each ex-serviceman a pocket watch and we can assume that Jim was among the recipients. The villagers then proceeded to dance the night away and the whole event concluded with a magnificent fireworks display.

The celebrations at an end, life in Bashall Eaves gradually returned to normality. Charles Gordon Lee decided to leave Backridge, and take his wife Lily and son Jack back to the family mansion in Birkenhead. The Lee family departed from Bashall Eaves soon after.

John and Jim Dawson

Almost inevitably, another cloud appeared to be looming on the horizon. It was becoming evident to the family that all was not well with Jim Dawson. His sisters considered that his actual personality had been changed by his wartime experiences. A concerned Polly commented that, *"He returned from the war a changed man. He became wilder"*.

What had actually happened to Jim while on active service is unknown as he always refused to talk about that period in his life. This was a very common reaction amongst those who served in the trenches. Probably it arose from the idea that unless you had actually been there and experienced the scale of the horrors witnessed by these men, any description was rendered pointless and somehow even crass. No account would ever be able to convey the gut-wrenching reality. To talk about it would be to remember. And the last thing most of these men wished to do was remember.

Whatever the cause, Jim began to act in a manner which the family considered unusual and unacceptable. He is said to have periodically lost interest in the farmwork and indeed life generally. It seems likely that he was suffering from bouts of depression brought on by post-traumatic stress disorder. These persisted on and off for some years until his death in 1934.

It is possible that Jim, unbeknown to the rest of the family, may have confided in his brother, for John seems to have maintained patience and understanding as far as his younger brother's lapses were concerned. Indeed in 1920 the two of them went into partnership and ran the Bashall Hall estate in tandem as Dawson Brothers. John saw to all the buying and selling of stock for the farm, while Jim ran the farm itself. Polly assisted her two brothers by keeping the books in order and keeping house for them.

Apart from Jim's occasional lapses into lethargy, things went fairly well for the Dawsons at Bashall Hall for the next few years. John and Jim's social lives at that time consisted of drinking in their local alehouses, The Red Pump at Bashall Eaves and the Edisford Bridge Hotel on the Clitheroe road. The two brothers also organised shooting parties for their farming friends. Indeed most of their social life centred on farming and farm-related activities. John's particular passion was for breeding and showing

Old English Game Bantams, and when only 18 years old he was invited to be a judge at the Crystal Palace show in 1897. On this occasion, as the youngest judge in the history of the show, he was invited to shake hands with Winston Churchill. This was always a source of great pride to him. Jim shared John's interest in bantam breeding to some extent, but his older brother was by far the more experienced of the two and his services as a judge at poultry shows were always in great demand.

The two brothers attended the cattle sales at Clitheroe Auction Mart on a regular basis. These were social as well as business occasions. Markets gave farmers a chance to catch up on local news and the latest gossip in the farming fraternity and it was a chance for friends to exchange family news. Clitheroe Auction Mart, where John and Jim Dawson sized up the cattle and bartered and chatted, is no longer held in the middle of Clitheroe, its site now being occupied by the stall market. However the auction mart is still very much in business on its new site on the outskirts of the town, where it was re-opened as The Ribblesdale Agricultural Centre by Baroness Trumpington on 26th August 1988.

While John and Jim were successfully running Bashall Hall Farm together, their younger brother Harry had also been doing very well for himself at Backridge. Indeed such was his acute business acumen that in 1925 he was able to sell out and retire at the remarkably early age of 37. Harry built his own bungalow, stone by stone, in the nearby village of Waddington, where Henry VI had sought refuge during the Wars of the Roses. Here Harry took up residence with his wife Maggie and two year old son Howard. His sister Annie joined the rest of the family at Bashall Hall.

One particularly vivid personal memory of Harry Dawson lingers in my mind. On one occasion, when I was very young, I was taken by my parents to visit him in Waddington. Harry came outside the bungalow to greet us, bent down and said to me kindly, "Hello. Do you like ice cream?"

"Yes," I lisped winningly. Since he had brought the subject up, I expected a choc ice or similar treat to be offered to me.

Harry thereupon straightened up smartly, pointed down the road and said, *"Well, there's a shop down there where you can buy one."* He then marched off into the house without a backward glance. Harry did not manage to retire at the age of 37 by buying ice creams for little girls.

Jim and his Women

Tragic news arrived at Bashall Hall in 1927 when the family learned of the death of Felix Dawson, who died of peritonitis in Australia where he had emigrated in 1910 shortly after his brother William. At the same time, Jim Dawson again suffered some sort of breakdown or serious illness - or at least this is how it was described by his sister Polly - it is difficult to make out exactly what went wrong in Jim's life in 1927. Polly Pickles said that this 'breakdown' again manifested itself by making him indifferent to his business. He would stay out until the early hours of the morning. Come the next morning he would stay in bed often until the afternoon and many times into the evening, even asking for meals to be brought upstairs for him. In the evening, he would then get out of bed, wash himself and go out again for the night without going near the barn to look at the stock or see to the farm work. It got to the stage where this was happening at least two or three times a week.

Jim's sisters Polly and Annie let Jim see that they did not approve of his behaviour, although they never openly quarrelled with him about it. Polly interpreted Jim's behaviour, as we have seen, as extreme depression and loss of interest in life. It seems just as reasonable to suppose, on the evidence available, that he was concentrating his energies on something he found considerably more interesting than the farm. Presumably a woman had come onto the scene. The sisters must surely have realised this. Polly said that she knew that he went to the Edisford Bridge Hotel when he went out at night, but that Jim never told them where he went after closing time or who he had been with. This should surprise nobody - Jim was never by any means a talkative person at the best of times, and we can be sure that he would not consider his amatory adventures a fit conversational subject for his sisters' ears. Without a doubt he would consider it to be none of their concern in any case.

Jim has always been portrayed as a quiet bachelor who expressed very little interest in women. Closer investigation has indicated that this was far from the case and he actually seems to have been quite a ladies' man.

By 1927 Jim Dawson had become a good-looking man with an extremely strong and muscular physique. While only 5' 5" tall which may seem short by today's standards, this was not considered to be particularly small by the local standards of the day. Jim was an exceptionally quiet and even-tempered man and seems to have been very much the 'strong, silent' type. He did not speak with a strong regional accent. Indeed in contrast to his portrayal in the media, Jim Dawson was well-spoken and refined.

Men and women seem to have had very different perceptions of this quiet bachelor farmer. His nephew Jack Lee describes him as having been 'really quite morose and dull' and cannot remember ever having seen him smile. This was probably because Jim did not bother to waste his smiles on seventeen year old nephews, or any other males come to that. For female relatives remember hearing stories of a very different Jim Dawson. When he walked into a room, he would immediately be surrounded by a crowd of women, and female opinion was that he was a 'very handsome man'. He obviously had the sort of charm totally lost on men and this can only be the quality that is sex appeal. It was certainly the women of the neighbourhood, rather than the men, who were the most distressed when he died in 1934.

The likelihood is therefore that Jim was out all night tiring himself out with the local ladies. It should perhaps be mentioned also that he does not seem have been in the best of health. He was suffering to some extent from inflammation of the kidneys, which may certainly have contributed to his low energy levels. Indeed his conduct at this time probably stemmed not from one specific cause, but from a combination of several.

Jim Dawson continued to stay out all night and neglect the farm on and off for the next few years. Who he was meeting at this time is unclear. In 1929, however, one of his lady friends finally emerged from the shadows. Her name was Lily Barker.

Lily Barker

Jim's girlfriend, Lily, was a married woman who had at some point separated from her husband, who remains a shadowy figure to this day. She worked as a barmaid at the Hodder Bridge Hotel, not far from Bashall Eaves, which was at that time run by the Greenwoods. Lily did not live at the public house, but had lodgings with a couple called Wrigley in Brownlow Street, Clitheroe. Mr. and Mrs. Wrigley were employed by Dr. Cooper, the Dawson family's physician.

Jim often visited Lily at her lodgings, but the Wrigleys maintained that the two love birds had never slept together in their house, all their 'courting' being done outside. They insisted that whenever Jim stayed the night, he slept with Mr Wrigley, thus defeating the whole object, one would have thought. Jim was also in the habit of meeting Lily at the Commercial Hotel in Clitheroe, situated in Russell Street (now part of Whalley Road). They also canoodled at the Edisford Bridge Hotel, one of Jim's favourite watering holes and where he spent the evening on the night he was shot five years later.

According to Lily herself, Jim took her to the cinema or theatre two or three times a week. In spite of its relatively small size, the town of Clitheroe could boast three cinemas. The courting couple were able to choose from The Grand in York Street (temporarily closed), The Palladium (on the site of the present Tesco) and the King Lane Picture Hall. Jim probably steered Lily firmly away from the King Lane cinema on May 26th 1929 as it was showing Alfred Hitchcock's *"The Farmer's Wife"*. I doubt Jim would have wanted to give Lily any ideas in that direction. He might have considered more suitable a film showing at the Palladium on 21st June. This had the delightful title, *"Plastered in Paris"*, and was, apparently, *"A roaring riotous rhapsody of rifts with the Riffs. A Harum Scarum comedy of two clowns in a desert, that would crack the enamel off the face of the Sphinx"*.

The nearest theatres were to be found in the town of Blackburn. At the Theatre Royal Jim and Lily might have enjoyed The Denville Players' production of *"Lawful Larceny"* or they may have attended a performance of *"The Happy Ending"* at Blackburn's other theatre, The Grand.

Needless to say there was no prospect of a happy ending for Jim and Lily, for the budding romance very soon hit the rocks. The reasons for this are unclear. Jim may have tired of her, or alternatively, as a married woman and mere barmaid, Jim's sisters may have considered her an unsuitable companion for their brother. Lily didn't give up without a fight however, and there are reports of her trying to force her way into Bashall Hall to find Jim, only to be repulsed by members of his family. Eventually, however Lily Barker was obliged to give up on Jim as a bad job. She left Clitheroe in 1930 and moved to Colwyn Bay in North Wales. Whether or not she was ever reconciled with her estranged husband is unknown.

Lily Barker seems to have been left with feelings of some bitterness towards Jim and his family. She stated five years later, *"I cannot think of anyone who would be jealous of my brief liaison with Mr. Dawson, but if there was anyone it would be his own sister!"* This certainly seems to indicate that one of Jim's sisters was behind the breakdown of Jim and Lily's relationship. Polly and Annie no doubt adored him (most women did) and it is possible that their attitude towards him was both over-protective and over-possessive. The implication is more sinister, of course, and I am quite sure this was exactly what Lily Barker intended.

No doubt Jim speedily consoled himself elsewhere, and life again returned to a semblance of normality for a while.

Lily and Jack Lee

In 1931, John and Jim Dawson gained two more dependants at Bashall Hall for it was in that year that their sister Lily lost her husband, Charles Gordon Lee. Poor Lily had not been having a good time of it since leaving Backridge back in 1919.

On her husband's return from the war, the family had removed to the family mansion "Wharfedale" in Prenton, Birkenhead. The Lee family traded as silk merchants, owned a gentleman's outfitters, Hope and Lee, and were extremely prosperous. Life rapidly became unbearable for Lily Lee. In spite of having a bevy of servants at her beck and call, Lily's mother-in-law behaved like all the ugly sisters rolled into one, and treated Lily, who was a gentle soul, like Cinderella. While Lily did not appreciate being treated like a slave, she had no fairy godmother waiting in the wings to wave a magic wand and so had to put up with it.

The situation was hardly improved by an incident involving her husband's brother, Kenneth. Kenneth Lee had been in Canada on business when war broke out, and joined the 205th Canadians - "The Tigers". During the war he found himself trapped in a tent for three months in a violent snowstorm, and as a result had become mentally unstable. During one of his seizures, poor Kenneth became so disorientated that he attacked his brother Charles Gordon with an axe. This proved the final straw. Life in Birkenhead had become not only uncomfortable for Lily Lee, but also physically dangerous for the whole family.

Charles Gordon, Lily and their son Jack fled from Wharfedale. For a few months they struggled in a first floor flat with no means of support. By now it was 1925 and life must have seemed bleak indeed. However, Lily's brothers at Bashall Hall were not prepared to see their sister in difficulties and came to her rescue. Jim and John Dawson arranged for the Lee family to return to Clitheroe and take up a smallholding at Up Brooks where they could keep cows, pigs and poultry. Lily gave birth to her second son, Ronald, while living at Up Brooks. During the birth, the cord became tightened around his neck and as a result the baby died aged just 8 days on October 14th 1928.

Three years later, tragedy struck the small family yet again. Charles Gordon Lee died in 1931 of double pneumonia, pleurisy and malaria (contracted in the Middle East during the war). Lily and Jack again found themselves in dire straits, and again Jim and John Dawson swooped to their aid. They invited their widowed sister and her son to live with them at Bashall Hall.

Lily and Jack were immensely relieved and grateful to have reached what they hoped would be a safe and secure berth at Bashall Hall. Jack Lee and his cousin Albert Pickles (who by this time was working on the estate with his uncles John and Jim) soon became inseparable. Albert was an extremely quiet, kind and inoffensive young gentleman, by all accounts. Not being accustomed to many treats in life, Jack Lee remembers being very touched when Albert gave him a chinchilla rabbit as a pet. Kind and gentle Albert may have been, but this did not prevent him being a deadly shot with both gun and catapult. He had been known to bag two rabbits with one shot, and used a catapult so powerful that even Jack (who practised bodybuilding and weightlifting) could not draw back the strings even an inch.

By 1931 the household at Bashall Hall accordingly comprised the two bachelor brothers John and Jim Dawson, their widowed sister Polly Pickles and her son Albert (aged 19) their widowed sister Lily and her son Jack (aged 15) and finally their unmarried sister Annie. The two Dawson brothers must have wondered rather ruefully how they had managed to acquire so many women and teenagers. In 1932, a 31 year old man called Tommy Kenyon was taken on as farm servant and joined the household at Bashall Hall.

Black clouds were beginning to gather on the horizon. Bashall Eaves might superficially have presented a picture of an idyllic rural community comparable only with J.R.R. Tolkien's 'The Shire'. Just beneath the surface, however, murky deeds were afoot. In or around October 1932, not only Jim but his brother John appear to have gone off the rails to such an extent that a local farmer felt compelled to remonstrate with them. In May 1934 Arthur Proctor stated, *"I have spoken to Jack and James Dawson about their conduct...About eighteen months or so ago James Dawson came out of a house in Russell Street about 4 a.m. and said, 'That's a dangerous place!' I spoke to James about his conduct. I told him he could not last long at that rate."* These were ominous and prophetic words indeed.

If the Dawsons of Bashall Hall thought they had been burdened with more than their fair share of difficulties in the past, they were mistaken. Their troubles were only just beginning, and Jim Dawson had less than two years left to live.

CHAPTER 3

Prelude to Murder
1933 – 1934

NEW Year festivities at Bashall Hall were a subdued event for Jim and his family in January 1933. For it had become clear that John Dawson was far from well and as the New Year got underway, his health took a marked turn for the worse. By this time, Jim had already engaged a male nurse, Mr. McLeod, to administer round-the-clock care for his ailing brother, but in spite of this, John never seemed to get any better. As well as worrying about John, Jim was also seriously concerned about the heavy expenses incurred by hiring the services of a live-in nurse. These proved to be a serious and long-term drain on the family finances. However, this could not be helped. Jim wanted nothing but the best for his sick brother.

In those dark, depressing days of January 1933, it was not only at Bashall Hall that health issues dominated people's thoughts, for a serious influenza epidemic was raging throughout the Clitheroe area. Many people were seriously ill, and spirits were generally low. The residents of Bashall Eaves cheered themselves up whenever they could by visiting neighbours, and carrying on with life as normally as possible. One such visit, however, came to a completely unexpected and violent conclusion when a friend of the Dawson family was attacked as he was leaving the grounds of Bashall Hall.

The Simpson Family and Mitton Church

On Tuesday, 3rd January, Tommy Simpson of Bashall Town Farm spent the evening at Bashall Hall chatting with Jim's sisters, and playing draughts with Jack Lee. Tommy was an old school friend, and the two neighbouring families socialised on a regular basis as their farms lay only a couple of hundred yards distant from each other.

The Simpsons were an extensive and confusing family. At least that was the considered opinion of the West Riding Constabulary during its investigation into Jim Dawson's murder a year or so later. The police officers virtually gave up in their attempts to grasp who precisely was related to whom, as it seemed to them that the Simpson family was related in one way or another to everyone in the district either by blood or by marriage.

Tommy Simpson was married to Kate, and Kate's sister Meta was married to Tommy's older brother William, who farmed at nearby Cheetall. Tommy and Kate had four children, the eldest of whom was a married son, Cyril (then 24 years old), who farmed nearby Brieryforth farm. They had three other unmarried children, Nancy, aged 20, (who worked as a domestic servant at Bashall Hall Cottage), Richard and Kathleen, all of whom lived with their parents at Bashall Town farm. Also living at Bashall Town at that time was Henry Bleazard, a nephew who also worked on the farm.

Tommy sat on the committee of the Clitheroe and Bowland branch of the National Union of Farmers, and both he and his wife Kate were particularly active members of their local church. Tommy served on the church council, (along with Harry Frankland, another of Jim's friends). He also acted as Sidesman and held the elected post of Diocesan and Ruri-decanal representative. The Simpson family worshipped at the charming old church of All Hallows, Mitton, which enjoys an elevated position overlooking the River Ribble about three miles from Bashall Eaves. The view from the churchyard can have few rivals for picturesque beauty, and it is here that many generations of the Dawson family have been buried.

A place of worship has stood on this site since about 1103, but the present building dates to the late thirteenth century, the tower having been added in the fifteenth. Surprisingly, no traces of funeral monuments associated with the powerful Talbot family of Bashall Hall are to be found within the church. Early tombs may have been destroyed during the building of the exquisite Shireburn Chapel, or the Talbots may for some reason have chosen to be buried on one of their other estates. Certainly some members of the family were buried at Stydd, a preceptory of the Knights Hospitallers, near Ribchester. In his will dated 1501 Nicholas Talbot from Bashall appointed a priest to sing for twelve months at Stydd Chapel, *"where fader and moder are buried."* Some later members of the Talbot family were buried at a Blackburn church.

Unlike Tommy Simpson and his other friends, Jim Dawson was not involved in church affairs. Indeed he never attended church, except for the obligatory weddings and funerals. This represented quite a break in tradition. In times past the Dawson men had always participated fully in church life and Jim's ancestors had filled the post of church-warden almost continually from 1752-1917. It is unclear why Jim (along with his brother John) should break so completely with family custom in this way. It is possible his religious views had been altered by his experiences in the trenches in the Great War. However the answer probably lies more in Jim Dawson's character, which was perhaps more retiring than that of his father Matthew, or his uncle Charles. Unlike them he seems to have had very little stomach for organising (or indeed taking any part in) local affairs, including those of the church.

Although Tommy Simpson of Bashall Town was a pillar of the local church and neither drank alcohol nor smoked, this did not seem to affect his relationship with Jim in the least, as far as we know. On 3rd January, therefore, Tommy spent a quiet and sociable evening at Bashall Hall with Jim's family as had been his custom for many years.

The Mysterious Assault

After bidding farewell to his hosts, Tommy walked up to the gate at the entrance to Bashall Hall's drive, and suddenly had the eerie feeling that he was being watched. He looked around but could see nothing moving as it was pitch black, blowing a gale and pouring with rain.

Tommy described what happened next to a local reporter:

"I opened the gate and as I stopped to pick up a milk can I had been carrying I was dealt a severe blow on the forehead with what appeared to be a heavy stick. I first thought it might be a falling bough, as half a gale was blowing, but when I recovered from the partial stunning I had received I saw a man, who had been skulking in the corner, climb a fence and run across the field towards the hall. I followed, but lost sight of him. I whistled and shouted as I ran down the field, and employees at Bashall Hall made their appearance. By this time, however, the man had got clean away. Afterwards I reported the matter to the police. My assailant was a man about 5 ft 8 in. in height, wearing a dark suit without overcoat. He was drenched with the heavy rain we had last night."

Tommy was at a complete loss to account for the attack. He commented, *"It was a shocking experience. I have never had anything like it before, and I hope I shall never have it again. I had a lump the size of an egg on my forehead last night, but it had disappeared this morning, though I had considerable pain, and did not sleep a wink all night."*

As no attempted robbery took place, we can probably assume that this was a spiteful attack by somebody nursing a grudge against Tommy Simpson of Bashall Town Farm. The assailant was evidently too cowardly to risk a face-to-face confrontation. He merely whacked Simpson over the head and then ran away into the dark, wet and windy night. Tommy reported the strange incident to the police, yet little attempt seems to have been made either to investigate the crime, or enquire into the motivation behind the malicious assault. The police merely *'kept a sharp lookout on the roads leading into the town and scoured the country lanes"*, almost as if they expected the assailant to be wandering conveniently around the countryside with a handy placard on his back reading, **'IT WOZ ME WOT DID IT'** in big black letters. Needless to say, no trace of Tommy Simpson's assailant was ever found. Tommy evidently suffered no lasting ill-effects, for three days later he and his wife Kate were to be found giving a recitation at Mitton Church.

Nevertheless the incident led to much local speculation and comment, and was recalled with curiosity a year or so later when Jim Dawson also suffered what seemed to be a random attack bearing some similarities to that perpetrated upon his friend and neighbour Tommy Simpson. Jim, of course, was not as lucky as Tommy Simpson, for in his case the night attack eventually proved to be deadly.

A few days after Simpson was ambushed at Bashall Hall, Lily Lee was walking to catch a bus to Clitheroe when a man called William Chew, who worked at Bashall Town Farm, joined her. Chew walked along with Lily and the subject of the assault came up in conversation. Chew said to her, *"The wrong chap was hit."* Lily turned to look at him, feeling scared, whereupon Chew attempted to reassure her by adding, *"It wasn't intended for anyone belonging to you, Mrs Lee."* This, of course, was hinting strongly that Chew knew the identity of the assailant, or thought that he did. It is a pity that he did not elaborate, and tell Lily who the blow **was** intended for.

Tommy Kenyon, Jim Dawson's farmhand at Bashall Hall at the time of the murder, relaxes by Bashall Brook in 1934.
Photo: family archive

Another episode involving William Chew may possibly be linked to the mystery attack. However it is unfortunately unclear from the police records whether this incident happened before or after the attack on Simpson took place. Annie Dawson and her sister Lily Lee were travelling home to Bashall on the local bus. At Bashall Road End, the driver called, *"Bashall Town"* and stopped the bus. William Chew, who was sitting with Tommy Kenyon, piped up, *"Bashall Town, what a hell of a shop!"* (This was presumably a quaint local insult of some sort in the 1930s.)

A few days later, Annie Dawson went to visit the Simpsons at Bashall Town, where Chew was employed. Mrs Simpson said that Tommy Kenyon had 'made use of' this remark on the bus. Annie put her right and said, *"It was not Kenyon, but Chew."* William Chew was subsequently sacked from Bashall Town as a result of his comment. Jim Dawson then became upset with his sister Annie, who said, *"My brother James complained to me of being the cause of him (Chew) having been discharged, as my brother had been drawn into the affair. My brother disliked any trouble."*

Tommy Kenyon, who had been on the bus with Chew when he made the offending remark, had come to live and work at Bashall Hall a year or so before. Kenyon had his own private little feud with his neighbour Tommy Simpson of Bashall Town. The root cause of all the animosity is unclear, but may have had something to do with Kenyon's relationship with Simpson's eldest daughter, Nancy. According to Tommy Kenyon himself, in Yorkshire TV's "The Village That Wouldn't Talk", Simpson "went for him" one night outside the barn at Bashall Town. He said that he always carried a stick with which to defend himself in case he was pestered by anybody.

As Kenyon passed the barn, Simpson came out of a stable and spotted him. Simpson's wife Kate exclaimed, *"That's him, Tommy. Get him!"*

Kenyon's response was, *"Right, I'll get thee first!"*

Simpson attempted to wrest the stick from Kenyon. These two full-grown men then proceeded to grapple each other to the ground, where they rolled around fighting. Kenyon commented that they didn't hurt themselves really, "just a scar or something of that sort", (which sounds pretty serious to me) and thereafter the two men had nothing but black looks for each other.

It has recently been suggested by a local that Tommy Kenyon might have been Tommy Simpson's unidentified assailant on 3rd January. By his own admission he always

The Dawson and Simpson ladies socialising at Bashall Town circa 1930. Nancy Simpson is in the top row on the left. Lily Dawson is fourth from the left in the middle row and on her right stands Kate Simpson, the wife of Tommy Simpson. Annie Dawson is seated in the foreground on the left. *Photo: family archive*

carried a stick, and the man in question was seen running towards Bashall Hall, where Tommy Kenyon lived and worked. Unfortunately Jack Lee's memory for once fails him, and he cannot recall Kenyon's movements on the night in question. Yet if Tommy Kenyon was indeed the mystery man concerned, then why did Simpson never suggest him as a possible suspect, bearing in mind that the two men disliked each other so much? A possible explanation is that Simpson did not wish to accuse Kenyon openly to the police because he would not wish to make trouble for his friend Jim Dawson who was Kenyon's boss. It is all very odd and without further evidence, the identity of Tommy Simpson's assailant must remain a mystery.

The above episodes go some small way towards illustrating the intricate relationships and petty quarrels festering deep within the deceptively peaceful farming community of Bashall Eaves in the year prior to the murder of Jim Dawson. Without a doubt, we are merely scratching the surface here. We have to ask ourselves; how many other deceptively trivial squabbles and jealousies which went unreported at the time eventually erupted into physical violence?

The Death of John Dawson

Towards the end of January 1933, Clitheroe and the surrounding area was hit by an earthquake powerful enough to throw furniture across rooms, and the people of Bashall Eaves must have wondered what had hit them. First they had been faced with a 'flu epidemic, then a mysterious assault and now an earthquake. What next was in store? The answer came two months later when the entire area was blanketed beneath 16 foot snowdrifts in March. Mother Nature appeared to be having a nervous breakdown.

Throughout this freezing month, John Dawson became progressively weaker. As the month of April commenced and the weather improved, it became clear that the warmer conditions were not helping and that he was not long for the world. To the sorrow of the whole family, John died in his own bed at Bashall Hall on 10th April.

His funeral was held on the 24th and the interment took place in Mitton churchyard.

Devastated by the loss of his much-loved brother, Jim immediately had to come to terms with taking overall charge of the Bashall Hall estate. He also had to cope with his new role as head of the household and assuming responsibility for the welfare of his two widowed sisters and their sons, and his unmarried sister Annie. And as if this were not enough, Jim also had the worry of dwindling family funds. He must at this time have felt as if the weight of the whole world was resting on his shoulders.

Having little choice in the matter, he shouldered his responsibilities and the family soldiered on.

The Summer of '33 - Poachers and Pig Races

After the earthquakes and heavy snow earlier in the year, the summer of 1933 proved to be an excellent one. The good weather tempted everyone outdoors. Unfortunately this included poachers, and on July 29th four men were arrested for poaching and assault in Bashall Eaves. These men, all of whom were from Nelson and Colne (some eleven miles away), were armed with a twelve-bore shot gun and a .410 rifle. On being alerted to their presence by the sound of gunfire, David Montgomery, the gamekeeper of the Worsley-Taylor estate, made the mistake of confronting the poachers. He was knocked down, surrounded by the men and repeatedly punched and kicked while on the ground. All four poachers were later fined £5 for assault, and various amounts for the offence of poaching. The impression has often been given that the Bashall Eaves area was an isolated place, where the sight of strangers was a rare one. However, visitors from miles around visited the local pubs, and it seems that poachers also would travel miles to pursue their illicit hunting activities. Bashall Eaves in the early 1930s was not really as cut off and isolated as the media would have us think.

Now that his more forceful older brother had died, Jim began to emerge from beneath his shadow. During the summer of 1933 he appeared to take a more active role in the local community. For the first time we see his name appearing in local newspaper

Jim's older brother and business partner, John Dawson, with one of his horses circa 1919. *Photo: family archive*

BASHALL EAVES & BROWSHOLME AGRICULTURAL & HORTICULTURAL SOCIETY

SHOW

will be held at Bashall Eaves on **SATURDAY, AUGUST 19th**
Excellent Classification for Cattle, Sheep, Poultry, Eggs, Bread, Horticulture. Stock Judging by the Young Farmers. Open events—**Horse sports** and **Tug-of-War, Pig Race, Foot Racing,** three classes, **Sheep Classes.** SHEEP DOG TRIALS open to Old Clitheroe Union. **ALL ENTRIES Close** on Saturday, August 12th. Special Attraction of Young Farmers Calves. **Schedules** may be obtained from the Secretary, ED. NEWHOUSE, Old Vicarage Farm, Bashall Eaves, Clitheroe.

Admission to Show Ground, 1/- all day

A **DANCE** in the ASSEMBLY ROOM after Show from 8-0 to 11-30 p.m. and also on **Monday** from 8 p.m. to 2 a.m. Buses will run every few minutes from Clitheroe Station and will also run from Bashall Eaves after the Dances on Saturday and Monday.

An advertisement for
Bashall Eaves Show, August 1933
Photo: Clitheroe Advertiser and Times

reports as he acted as judge in farming competitions and participated in events at the local agricultural show. He was no doubt expected to step into John's shoes, and this cannot have been easy for him, being a shy and retiring sort of man.

The annual Bashall Eaves Show was held on 19th August in glorious weather in its usual field near the Red Pump Hotel. Admission to the show ground cost one shilling for the whole day and people flocked from far and wide to take part in the event. As well as prize-giving for the best cattle and sheep in the area, attractions included sheepdog trials and several sporting activities such as a tug-o-war. In the horse racing events, Jim took part in the "Farmers' Trot", coming in second to T. Metcalf, and "The Farmers' Gallop" when he was again pipped at the post by Mr. Metcalf.

Never having attended an agricultural show, the name of one particular race which took place in 1933 delighted and intrigued me. This was "The Pig Race For Ladies". Its very title caused my imagination to run riot. Did ladies take pigs to the show with them and then race them? Or did the local ladies put on pig masks, perhaps, and race themselves, pretending to be pigs? I soon learned to my disappointment that it was nothing quite so exotic. A young greased pig was brought to the grounds in a van, tied up in a sack and then let loose in a field. The local women then attempted to catch it. This generally took quite a while, as the pig often escaped the confines of the field and ran off into the distance, with the ladies in hot pursuit. On this particular occasion, the "Pig Race for Ladies" was won by Mrs. F. Pye.

After the show, a dance was held in the Bashall Eaves Assembly Room and special buses were laid on to ferry people to and from Clitheroe and the surrounding areas.

The Edisford Bridge Hotel - Ghosts and Lotteries

Jim's social life at this time continued to revolve around his nights out at the Edisford Bridge Hotel, where he walked for a drink virtually every evening after work. Two other farming friends* were regularly to be found in the pub, these being George Towler of Edisford Bridge Farm (next to the pub) and Harry Frankland of Edisford Hall Farm close by. As we have said, Tommy Simpson of Bashall Town was not a drinker, while Jim's other old school chum Bill Eccles tended to favour The Red Pump Hotel in Bashall Eaves over the hostelry at Edisford Bridge (as did Albert Pickles). It should not be assumed that the clientele of the Edisford Bridge Hotel was made up exclusively of local people. Reports in the local newspaper make it clear that the pub was often frequented by customers from as far away as Nelson, Colne and Blackburn (all approximately eleven miles distant). This was a popular pub.

Little appears to be known of the history of the Edisford Bridge Hotel as it stands today, but an inn of some sort has no doubt been present on or near its site for centuries. Edisford (or Eddisford, as it is written in the 30s) itself is thought to mean 'the nobleman's ford', and has a rich and colourful history. In 1138 King David of Scotland engaged and defeated the forces of King Stephen here during the period of English history known, with good reason, as The Anarchy.

A century or so later, a leper hospital of St. Nicholas was founded at Edisford for the exclusive use of the township of Clitheroe. Its traditional site (and probably the correct one) is at Edisford Hall, which was the home of the Frankland family in the early 1930s. Entry into a leper house was a sentence of living death for those unfortunate enough to catch the disease, for, as the sufferers entered the hospital, they underwent a symbolic funeral in which they were declared dead to the world. Thereafter they were obliged to wear distinctive dress and handed a warning rattle or bell to warn others of their presence. These unfortunate lepers trudged down the same road along which, 700 years later, Jim Dawson strode briskly every evening for a night out at the Edisford Bridge Hotel.

A bridge has existed at Edisford since early mediaeval times. Indeed until the seventeenth century, Edisford Bridge was the only bridge over the Ribble above Preston, and its original name was The Bridge of Ribble. It was seriously damaged by flooding in 1339, and tolls were subsequently collected on various commodities, as they were transported across the bridge from Lancashire into Yorkshire, in order to raise money for repairs. Some of the items upon which tolls were levied were surprisingly luxurious and exotic, including almonds, cumin, sea fish, honey, figs and wine. Traders in cloth from as far away as Galway, the Isle of Man and Ireland utilised this route and an inn would certainly have been sited close to the bridge in medieval times to take full advantage of these tired and thirsty trading folk.

The present inn probably dates back to the seventeenth or eighteenth century. In Jim Dawson's day it had the reputation of being haunted. One lady and her husband, who lived there for several years, were constantly disturbed by the sound of a child crying.

---

*Whether any of these men can accurately be described as 'friends' is debatable. The term is used throughout merely as a convenient one for men with whom Jim socialised more closely than with others. As far as the family was aware, Jim Dawson did not really have a 'best friend' to whom he might have confided his innermost feelings and secrets.

In one particular bedroom, they said, furniture constantly moved around, and in another room a light could never be kept burning at certain times of year. The figure of a woman also startled the residents as she drifted around the building, and it was thought that the haunting was caused by a woman having murdered a child in the house sometime in the past. The present landlord does not appear to be aware of any spirits other than those on sale behind the bar.

Presumably oblivious to the resident ghosts, Jim Dawson had a few drinks and played dominoes with his farmer friends nearly every night, and also took part in what seems to have been another regular activity at his favourite public house. This was known as a "lottery"*. There appear to have been two distinct lotteries run at the Edisford Bridge Hotel. One was run quite openly by the licensee, Jack Barnes, and involved the customers bringing in a parcel, which was raffled at a later date. The profits were put aside to provide a good dinner at the pub for those having taken part by buying the raffle tickets. Another lottery was run by a committee made up of a particular group of customers, (one of whom may have been Jim himself) which seems to have been a more secretive affair. This second lottery involved the selling of raffle tickets for particular prizes such as turkey, geese and chocolates.

Apart from regular visits to the pub, what sort of lifestyle did Jim Dawson and his rest of his family lead at this time? Fortunately, my father Jack Lee is able to recall the early 1930s in surprising detail and his memories paint a vivid picture of everyday life at Bashall Hall in the year or so prior to the murder of Jim Dawson.

Everyday Life at Bashall Hall

Jack remembers the time he spent at Bashall Hall with great nostalgia and affection. He lost his heart to the old Talbot mansion as a teenager and the love affair has not diminished one jot over the past seventy years. Whenever I complain about my house being too cramped and noisy (which is often) my father will exclaim enthusiastically and unreasonably, *"Buy Bashall Hall! You'd like it there. It's nice and big and peaceful!"*

Bashall Hall had for many years been rented out to tenants by the owners, the Worsley-Taylor family, as two separate units. One unit comprised Bashall Hall proper, including the farm estate, and the other was Bashall Hall Cottage. This was not a separate cottage, but the West Wing of Bashall Hall itself. The Dawsons lived in the main part of the house, while the self-contained "cottage" was rented by a barrister, Mr. Ben Ormerod and his wife, who employed Nancy Simpson of Bashall Town as their domestic servant.

As electricity had yet to be installed, the only form of lighting in the hall was provided by candles and a spirit lamp. The Dawsons did not own a telephone, and in emergencies used the 'phone next door at Bashall Hall Cottage belonging to their more

---

* Such lotteries were made illegal in 1934. The licensee of the Edisford Bridge Hotel was subsequently prosecuted for allowing his premises to be used for 'illegal lotteries'.

prosperous neighbours, the Ormerods. In order to obtain water, it was necessary for someone to go down to Bashall Brook and use the pump near the bridge to draw it up. The water thus obtained was invariably teeming with insect life and required sieving before it could be used for drinking, washing or cooking purposes.

There was no bathroom at Bashall Hall when Jack Lee lived there. Baths were taken in the kitchen in front of the fire. A large tin bath was carried in for the purpose, into which was poured water drawn from the brook and heated over the fire. Neither did the house have inside toilet facilities. The toilet was housed in a stone building situated in a field called The Copy*, adjacent to the house. As there was no piped water, the toilet did not have a cistern or flushing mechanism, and the facilities consisted of a wooden seat placed over a bucket. It was the job of the unfortunate Albert Pickles to empty the bucket into the midden (or rubbish heap) at the top end of The Copy. Should anyone be 'caught short' in the middle of the night, chamber pots were placed handily under the beds to remove the necessity of leaving the house.

Jack enjoyed whiling away any spare time in The Barracks, which was utilised for several purposes. In the lower storey, haymaking machinery was stored to the left; while on the right the farm horses and bulls were tethered. Hay was stacked upstairs, and the rest of the space on the upper storey lay vacant. Here Jack began to practise his lifelong hobby of body-building and weight-lifting. Albert Pickles sometimes joined in, along with other young men from the local farming community.

---

* So-called because it was originally a coppice used to produce young and pliable wood.

Bashall Hall, built by the Talbots and farmed by members of the Dawson family from the eighteenth century until 1972. This photograph was taken in 1934, the year Jim Dawson died.
Photo: J. G. Lee

Plain, good food was available. Polly tended a kitchen garden, which faced the house, and here she grew vegetables and flowers. She also produced her own butter and cheese. Meat was delivered to the house by Jack Lofthouse, a local butcher from Low Moor in Clitheroe. The hall had its own orchard to provide fresh fruits such as damsons, which were then bottled for later use. If any other shopping was required, then Polly as housekeeper was obliged to walk two miles into Clitheroe, and then two miles back carrying heavy bags. She was even expected to cart the extremely large and heavy batteries for the family radio all the way from Clitheroe on foot. The eventual provision of a bus service in 1934 must have proved quite a relief to her.

A 1980s view of the Georgian summer house (or gazebo) at Bashall Hall, probably built by the Ferrers family. The land in front of the summer house, across which the calf is marching, is the field known as The Copy.
Photo: N. J. Cobban

The usual meal at Bashall Hall comprised plain roast meat with potatoes and vegetables. Polly also insisted upon serving up sago pudding at virtually every mealtime, which Jack Lee hated. She also persisted in offering him large slices of seed cake, which he utterly detested. (He didn't much care for roast meat and potatoes, either, come to that.) His poor Auntie Polly must have been at her wit's end wondering what she could offer this choosy young person that he would actually enjoy eating. In the absence of any alternative, she doggedly continued to serve up meat and vegetables, sago and seed cake.

Jim Dawson did not own a car. Not many farmers could afford to run one at this time. One of the few who did own a car was Tommy Simpson of Bashall Town, and Harry Dawson, Jim's brother, was another. Colonel Parker of nearby Browsholme Hall in the Forest of Bowland preferred to stick to the old ways. He was often seen around the neighbourhood driving in style with his coach and horses. Jim himself couldn't run to a coach and four, but did own a pony and trap. Why Polly was not permitted to use it for her shopping trips in the days before a bus service is a bit of a mystery. Possibly Jim Dawson was not invariably kind and considerate towards his widowed sisters.

The family spent most of its time in the small kitchen, which was the warmest place in the house. This room was dominated by a large open fireplace, containing an oven, over which was suspended a clothes maiden for drying the washing. This could be raised to the ceiling by means of a pulley when not in use. A rocking chair was placed in front of the fireplace. Jack was often told the story of his great-grandfather, who used to hog the seat in front of the fire. Armed with a large stick, he would lash out indiscriminately at anyone else who had the temerity to approach the fire. A small dining table lay against one wall, where the family ate its meals. As it was too small for the whole family to sit around, people tended to eat their meals at different times.

Next door to the kitchen was the refectory (or dining room), containing an enormously long table, which was only used during haymaking time when temporary extra staff were engaged. Next to this was the Chill Room. In the absence of a refrigerator, milk and other dairy items were stored here and kept cool on stone blocks. The sitting room was also located next to the dining room, with a small (and somewhat redundant) "Prayer Room" leading off it. This area was used only by Jack Lee and his cousin Albert Pickles. Jack had by this time left Clitheroe Royal Grammar School for Boys, and was attending Guests Business Training College, in Exchange Street, Blackburn. The Prayer Room was a handy and quiet place to study and here Jack struggled to master shorthand. His Auntie Polly was very considerate and often built a fire for her nephew in this little room so he would not feel cold when he was working.

The Great Hall, on the first floor, was not used as living space in the early 1930s. Where in times past the Ferrers family held their feasts and dances, now bats flourished in great numbers. Their dark wings festooned the ancient walls, casting misshapen shadows across the abandoned banqueting room, while their squeaks filled the air. It would be difficult to conjure up a more Gothic image. Jack Lee and Albert Pickles ignored the bats and played cricket in the Great Hall as it provided a large and enclosed space. I am assured that they never broke any windows (or hurt any bats). In later years, Albert kept bantam hens in cages there.

There were four bedrooms on the first floor. A small spare bedroom to the right was in later years converted into a bathroom. Facing this was Polly's room. To the left, up one step, was Lily Lee's room and at the far end of this room was a door leading to the fourth bedroom. This was where Annie slept in her magnificent four-poster bed. Jack remembers watching his Auntie Annie brushing her hair while sitting on the four poster getting ready for bed. He had never seen such long hair as hers, which swept the top of her thighs. Two further bedrooms were located on the second floor. In one of these slept Albert Pickles and Tommy Kenyon, the farmhand, while Jack Lee shared the other with his Uncle Jim. Nobody was required to share a bed at Bashall Hall.

While bats roosted unmolested on the walls of the Great Hall, other creatures made themselves heard in the bedrooms. Jack would lie in bed listening to strange noises emanating from the old walls – rustle, rustle, slither, slither – as the rats scuffled around in the wall cavities. Occasionally one would manage to scrabble its way to the top of the wall and then lose its footing and fall down to floor level again with a loud thud. This must have been somewhat disconcerting in the middle of the night. Surprisingly, none of these rodents was ever seen in the house by the family. (If any rat had the temerity to show its face outside, Albert shot it.)

As if the regular company of bats and rats were not quite enough, Jack experienced a close encounter with another wild creature one night when he was asleep in bed. He woke up with a start, and as his eyes accustomed themselves to the gloom he became aware of two enormous eyes staring at him from the bottom of the bed, and a feeling of pressure on his feet. *"What the hell is that?"* he wondered in some alarm, having watched several Boris Karloff films. The intruder turned out to be nothing more

The late medieval building known as The Barracks at Bashall Hall, taken in 1934. Tradition maintains that the Talbot family stationed its private army here in the fifteenth century.
Photo: J. G. Lee

sinister than 'a bloody great owl' which had flown in through the open window and chosen Jack as a handy perch. Having dislodged it from his feet, he proceeded to chase it round and round the bedroom. The bird proved extremely difficult to capture as Jack was doing his best not to injure it, and there was very little to get hold of as it was 'all feathers and no meat'. Eventually the doubtless stressed owl was evicted from the equally stressed Jack's room and it flew out of the open window into the blackness from whence it came. I invariably visualize this incident accompanied by a Hammer Horror soundtrack of wolves howling and a magnificent thunder storm raging around Bashall Hall.

Indeed living at Bashall Hall in those days must have felt much like participating in a horror film. Not being prone to flights of fancy, Jack tends to bellow, *"Rubbish!"* at such observations. He will never hear a word against his favourite house, and is even less impressed when faced with the suggestion that Bashall Hall might have been haunted. Then again, other Dawsons seem to disagree with him, and a family tradition maintained that the hall was haunted by the ghost of Henry VI. *"Mind the ghost!"* the Dawson men would roar mischievously after their new wives when they visited Bashall Hall for the first time, and were ascending the staircase alone.

The Barracks in about 1980, after some restoration work.
Photo: N. J. Cobban

Little Mary

Lily and Jack Lee, and Annie Dawson, would occasionally take a short break from life in Bashall Eaves to visit the seaside resort of Blackpool. These little holidays were spent with a relative, Mrs Mitchell, who owned a boarding house in the town. When in Blackpool, Annie often took the opportunity to consult a psychic and clairvoyant known as Little Mary.

Little Mary (so-called due to her diminutive height) was no tacky gypsy fortune-teller operating on the Golden Mile, but a cartomancer who made her predictions using an ordinary pack of cards (rather than a Tarot deck). Her clients suspected that she used the cards merely because it was expected, and in reality had no need of such visual tools. The readings were held in the small living room of her own house, which always had a strange odour as Little Mary smoked foul-smelling cigarettes called Sultans, which cost tuppence for ten. There was no set fee for the sitting, clients paying what they could afford. As well as predicting the future with uncanny accuracy, she also described past events in her clients' lives and it appears that she was never wrong.

Occasionally her predictions about the future, while precise, came to pass in rather an unexpected manner. A relative of the Dawson family called Gracie Hitchon, for example, was informed by Little Mary that while she worked up North at present, she would shortly be transferred down South. There she would meet a man 6' 4" tall called Bill, who would be either the manager or a shop walker and she would marry him within six months. Gracie became rather apprehensive. She had no desire to move down South and marry a gigantic Southerner. Her worries proved groundless. She worked for Littlewoods department store on the North Shore at Blackpool. Gracie was subsequently transferred to Littlewoods on the South Shore of the town, where she met a man who was indeed called Bill who was exactly 6' 4" tall. They were married three months later.

While Jack Lee may not be impressed with the idea of ghosts infesting his beloved Bashall Hall, the minute accuracy exhibited by Little Mary, including the furnishing of actual names, impressed him so much that in later years he occasionally consulted her himself when he was in Blackpool, taking his friends along with him. Little Mary even predicted her own death. At the end of what was to be his last reading, Jack said to her, *"I'm coming to Blackpool again in a few weeks' time. I'll come and see you then."*

Her reply was short and to the point. *"Don't bother,"* she said, *"I'll be dead"*. And indeed she was.

The Chestnut Tree Tragedy

What Jim Dawson thought about his family's visits to clairvoyants is not recorded. As a busy farmer, Jim had no time for holidays, and it is unlikely that he would have had much time for clairvoyants either. He had more than enough trouble with the present without wondering what the future would bring.

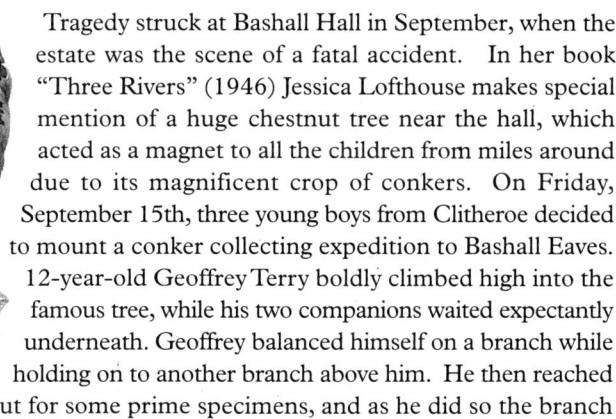

Tragedy struck at Bashall Hall in September, when the estate was the scene of a fatal accident. In her book "Three Rivers" (1946) Jessica Lofthouse makes special mention of a huge chestnut tree near the hall, which acted as a magnet to all the children from miles around due to its magnificent crop of conkers. On Friday, September 15th, three young boys from Clitheroe decided to mount a conker collecting expedition to Bashall Eaves. 12-year-old Geoffrey Terry boldly climbed high into the famous tree, while his two companions waited expectantly underneath. Geoffrey balanced himself on a branch while holding on to another branch above him. He then reached out for some prime specimens, and as he did so the branch on which he was standing splintered and broke. Geoffrey plunged 30 feet to the ground and landed in a bed of nettles.

The other two boys immediately ran to Bashall Hall where they told Annie Dawson and Jack Lee what had happened. Jack comforted the quiet and uncomplaining boy while the doctor and ambulance were called, and after treatment at the scene Geoffrey was rushed to Blackburn Royal Infirmary suffering from severe shock, cuts and bruises, a compound fracture of the thigh and a broken wrist. Five days later the poor lad died in hospital of septicaemia (blood poisoning). The Coroner commented that the blood poisoning was probably contracted when germs entered the thigh wound as he was lying under the tree. He added, somewhat insensitively, that Geoffrey was actually trespassing on Bashall Hall land at the time of the accident. Poor Geoffrey's sad and unexpected death shocked and upset the entire neighbourhood. The Dawson family was horrified that such a dreadful thing should have happened on their farm. While Bashall Hall was certainly no stranger to tragedy, the death of this young boy in September 1933 contributed a particularly poignant episode to its already chequered history.

As the dark days of winter approached, many people felt the need to have something to look forward to. Down at the Edisford Bridge Hotel, plans were afoot to hold a major 'lottery' dinner in March 1934. To give themselves plenty of time to raise funds, Jim and the other locals began to prepare their individual parcels which had to be worth about one shilling and sixpence. These would be raffled on each Saturday and Sunday night for the next few months. All those taking part in the proceedings also agreed to pay one shilling towards the cost of the dinner nearer to the time. The proceeds could then, as usual, be used to provide a really special get-together in the Spring. Jim Dawson decided that on this occasion his prize would be a parcel of cigarettes, and this was raffled to the assembled company in the Edisford Bridge Hotel just before Christmas.

If Jim reflected at all upon the events of the previous twelve months, he probably reached the conclusion that 1933 had been a year of very mixed fortunes. It had witnessed freak weather conditions and petty squabbles. It had also seen a mysterious attack and the death of a young boy - both taking place on his land - and most devastating of all, the blow of the untimely death of his brother John. On the other hand, the summer months had proved idyllic with Jim, for the first time, seeming to come out of his shell a little and beginning to take a more active part in local farming events. No doubt it was his fervent hope that 1934 would prove to be a more peaceful and less eventful year than 1933. This hope was not to be realised.

The Final Few Months - 1934

January 1934 saw little of moment happening in Jim Dawson's life as far as we can tell. Towards the end of February, however, Jim began to behave strangely. He reverted to his old habits of staying out all night, and remaining in bed until 3 o'clock in the afternoon. Even on a good day, he never rose before 9 a.m., and left all the feeding and care of the farm's cattle to Albert Pickles and Tommy Kenyon. The novelty of taking personal charge of the farm estate after his brother's death might perhaps have worn off. Jim may once again have been finding it all too much for him.

Throughout the months of January and February 1934, prizes in aid of the March 3rd lottery dinner continued to be raffled at the Edisford Bridge Hotel. Jim Dawson appears to have been exceptionally lucky in these raffles, winning numerous items including turkeys and boxes of chocolates. Jim's nephew, Jack Lee, while unaware of the lotteries taking place at the Edisford Bridge, does clearly remember his uncle carrying home one prize after another at this time.

However on 26th February, Jim informed Jack Barnes, the landlord that he would be unable to attend the dinner on 3rd March. He said, *"I shan't be able to come to the do on Saturday, Jack. I'm going to a farm sale at Worston. I'll pay my bob same as everybody else!"* Jim was referring to the shilling fee which each of those attending the dinner was paying to boost the proceeds of the raffles. He went on to say that he might pop in at about 9 o'clock after the farm sale had finished.

A day or so later, when Jim was (as usual) in the Edisford Bridge playing dominoes, a man called William Brayshaw came in enquiring after Jim's friend Harry Frankland of Edisford Hall farm. Jim eyed him with misgiving. The next evening he asked the landlord if he knew who the man was. When Jack Barnes said he did not, Jim filled him in and issued a warning. He said that he suspected Brayshaw of stealing prize-winning bantam hens from Bashall Hall and added, *"I don't think he is up to any good being around here."* Why Brayshaw had been asking for Harry Frankland is unknown.

After the exceptionally dry month of February, rain at last fell on March 2nd as the lambing season swung into high gear. On March 3rd, the night of the lottery dinner, Jim did not turn up all night. He was, however in the pub the following two evenings, and on one of these George Towler of Edisford Bridge Farm asked him, *"Did you go to the farm sale at Worston, Jim?"*

Jim replied, *"No, I didn't get there. I had other business on."* He did not specify what this business might have been.

When we consider that Jim had reverted to his previous habits of staying out all night and neglecting the farm business, this might indicate that he had taken up with a new girlfriend. Perhaps he missed the long-anticipated lottery dinner because he was 'on a promise', and had made use of the Worston farm sale as a handy and believable excuse to explain his absence.

It was at about this time that Harry Frankland claimed to have seen a stranger lurking suspiciously outside the Edisford Bridge Hotel. Frankland had popped in for a drink on a week night at about 8.45 p.m. As he was climbing the steps to the pub entrance, he happened to look back to the gate leading to the hotel croft. There he saw, clearly illuminated in the electric lamp, a man leaning on the gate and watching the hotel door. Frankland described him as being about 40 years old, clean-shaven and about 5' 8"- 5' 10" tall. He was dressed in a light grey raincoat and wearing a trilby hat. When the man became aware of Frankland's scrutiny, he quickly turned his face away from the light.

Jim appears to have been in a strange mood at this time and his normally even temper seems to have occasionally deserted him. This is illustrated by an unusual confrontation which took place between Jim and his nephews Albert Pickles and Jack Lee. As a change from playing cricket in the Great Hall, Jack and Albert decided to have a game in the open air. They chose as their pitch a field lying close to Bashall Brook known as The Holmes*. Later in the day, Jim buttonholed them in the kitchen angrily demanding to know what they thought they were doing playing cricket on grazing land. Jim was particularly attacking Jack in the argument, it would seem, and Albert Pickles fired up in his cousin's defence. Jack Lee remembers this incident very clearly, because it was so unlike his normally easy-going uncle to become so irate. He barely ever raised his voice. Indeed his farmhand Tommy Kenyon once commented that he had never once known Jim Dawson to lose his temper.

The Edisford Bridge Inn (formerly Hotel) 2004. Jim Dawson had a drink here nearly every evening, including the night he was shot.
Photo: author

---

* Meaning, aptly enough, 'riverside land'.

Jim was obviously troubled and upset about something. Whether it was caused by a woman or money worries is debatable, and it may have been both. He was unquestionably worried about the family finances at this time. He had recently lost a milk cow due to milk fever - a disaster in those days. Even more seriously, on Friday 9th March, the following legal notice referring to his brother John Dawson's estate appeared in the Clitheroe Advertiser and Times:

LEGAL NOTICES

RE: JOHN DAWSON, DECEASED

All Persons having claims against the estate of the above deceased late of Bashall Hall Farm, Bashall Eaves, who died on the 20th day of April, 1933, are requested to send particulars thereof;- and all persons owing monies should pay the Same to me the undersigned forthwith.

THOMAS J. BACKHOUSE
33 Richmond Terrace, Blackburn
Solicitor to the Executors

According to his sister Polly, Jim was extremely anxious about Jack's will, and told her that 'it could not be met'.

There remains little to record about the last week of Jim's life. A few days before he was shot, Jim entered into a partnership with his sister Polly and her son Albert Pickles to trade as Dawson Brothers at Bashall Hall Farm. Polly and Albert's names were duly placed in the rent book, alongside that of Jim himself.

On Friday, 16th March, Jim went for his usual drink at the Edisford Bridge Hotel, where he was seen outside the pub by Mr. and Mrs. Wrigley, the landlords of his old girlfriend, Lily Barker. On the evening of 17th March, Jim was again to be found in the pub, where he met Harry Frankland for a drink.

At about 6.30 p.m. on the ill-fated Sunday of 18th March 1934, Jim washed and dressed for what was destined to be his final night out at the Edisford Bridge Hotel. The resident spirits of Bashall Hall skittered uneasily as they watched Jim's preparations, and a frisson of apprehension quivered through the old building. For as Jim cast a last quick look at himself in the mirror before leaving, a mysterious individual was putting the finishing touches to his own secret and deadly plans for that evening.

CHAPTER 4

The Murder

AT about seven o'clock on that wild, dark and rain-swept evening of Sunday, 18th March 1934, Jim Dawson set out for his customary drink at the Edisford Bridge Hotel. For his night out Jim had chosen to wear a grey jacket and waistcoat over a woollen shirt, with a brown check overcoat to protect him from the foul weather. Finally, he donned his usual bowler hat. Jim left Bashall Hall by the back door and took the short cut across the field to Bashall Town, heading for the road to Clitheroe.

Back at the hall, the rest of the family members were in the kitchen wondering how to spend the evening. Albert Pickles, Jim's nephew, had taken one look at the weather and decided against his usual jaunt to meet friends at the Red Pump Hotel in Bashall Eaves. As he was nursing a cold, he thought an early night was probably the best thing for him. Albert suffered regularly from colds and usually treated himself by taking gruel. Neither was Jim's other nephew Jack Lee tempted to go out - he seldom did so - and tonight was no exception. Jack decided to spend the evening reading a novel. He would then catch up on some shorthand study in preparation for one of his final weeks at Guests Business College in Blackburn.

Jim's sisters Polly and Lily busied themselves in the kitchen. His other sister Annie was sleeping elsewhere that night. Brother Bob and his wife May often visited on Sunday evening with their two sons Maxwell and Charlie, but on this particular Sunday they were not expected. However, there was always more than enough for the sisters to do. The family switched on the wireless and settled down for a quiet night in, pursuing their various chosen activities.

Jim's farm labourer, Tommy Kenyon, had no intention of letting the weather interfere with his night out and when Albert said he was 'lying in' to nurse his cold, Tommy set out alone to see who was around at the Red Pump. As he walked along, Tommy might have reflected upon how seldom Jim joined him at this particular public house any more. This was due to an unfortunate incident some three years earlier, when Jim had been the victim of an abusive verbal attack by one Harry Leeming, necessitating intervention from the landlord.[*] Jim hated confrontation of any kind and now tended to steer clear of the Red Pump, apart from popping in very occasionally to have a drink with his old school friend Bill Eccles.

---

[*] The cause of this altercation is unknown

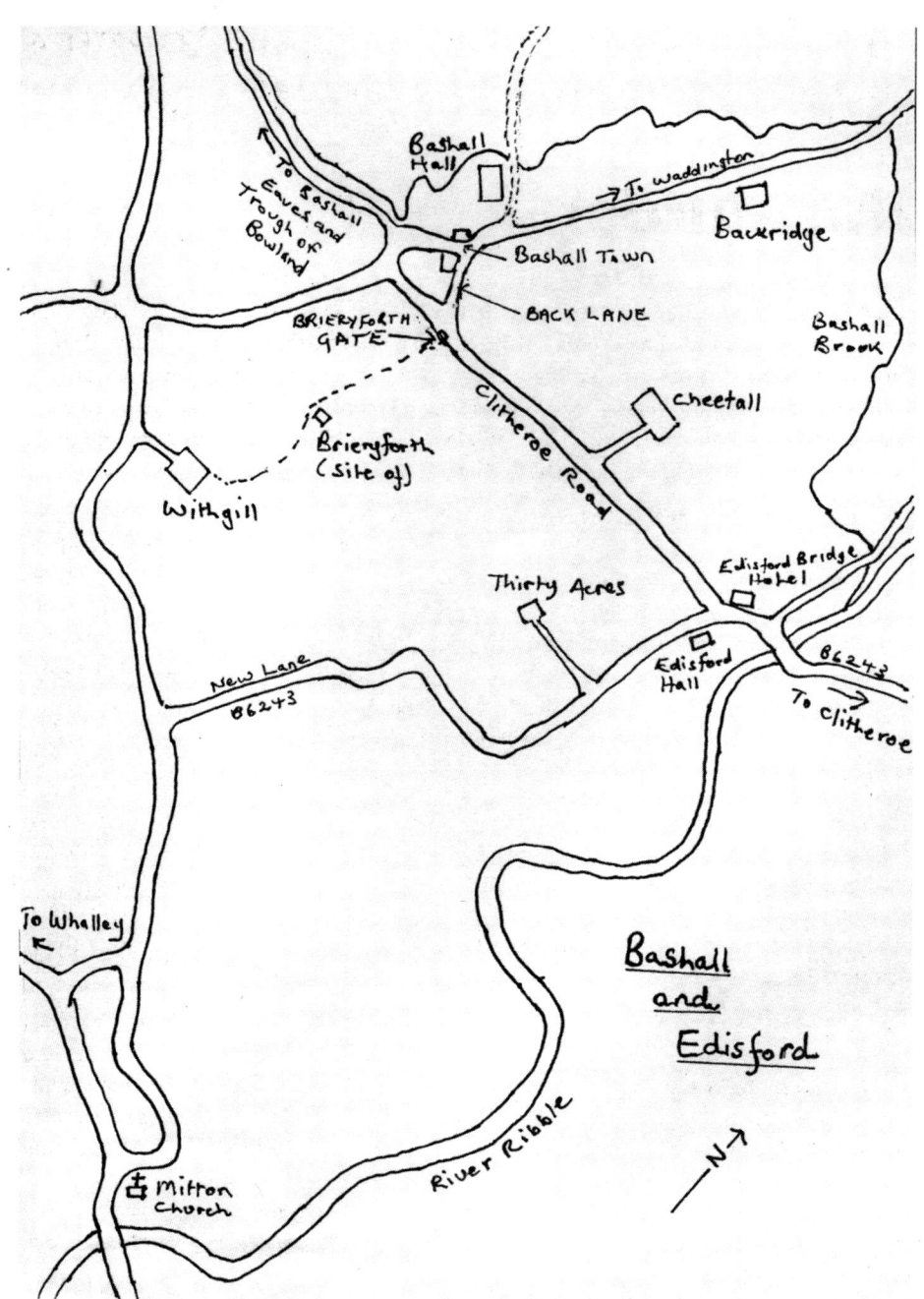

Location map of area.
Map based on Paths Around Pendle, courtesy of Duncan Armstrong and Associates, Padiham

The Final Night at the Edisford Bridge Hotel

Being a brisk walker, Jim arrived at the Edisford Bridge Hotel at about 7.15 p.m. He was greeted at the bar by Jack Barnes, the licensee. Jim ordered a glass of gin (a surprising drink, perhaps, for a Yorkshire farmer to choose) and the two men stood chatting about this and that for fifteen minutes or so. When he had finished his gin, Jim went into the taproom to see who else was in that night. He may have felt a little surprised and disappointed to find that his usual drinking buddies were absent. While we have seen that his friend Tommy Simpson of the neighbouring Bashall Town was not a drinking man, Jim might certainly have expected to see Harry Frankland of Edisford Hall Farm, who was a regular drinking companion, as was George Towler of Edisford Bridge Farm next door to the pub.*

Jim glanced round the room at the assembled company. He saw Matthew Hughes, a general workman at Withgill Farm near Mitton, Tom Brown and Hugh Priestly who both lived in Clitheroe, Dick and Clifford Thornber of Withgill Piggeries and Eziah Ireland of Henthorn. Also present were Thomas Hillary, James Parkinson, James Brown and a man called Edmundson. James Preston had chosen to sit by himself in the snug.**

Jim sat down next to Matthew Hughes, beside whom he remained seated all evening. Nobody was playing dominoes that night so the two men chatted generally about farming and football. At 8.10 p.m. Jim bought a pint for James Parkinson, a farm labourer, and during the course of the evening Jim himself had a further four drinks - two glasses of beer and two pints (which appear to be two different measures in 1934). Jim never drank excessively on his nights out. Tommy Kenyon commented in 1980, *"There weren't many farmers drunk - they were too greedy to go out and buy a gill or two!"* There do not appear to have been any disputes or quarrels and Jim himself commented later that the company was quite agreeable and that he did not have a wrong word with anyone†.

At about 8.50 p.m. the company began to break up as in those days the Edisford Bridge Hotel closed at 9 o'clock on Sunday. Some men left the pub to go to Clitheroe (where opening hours were longer) while others left by car. At about 9 o'clock, Jim decided it was time he also made a move. He bought a box of matches, put on his overcoat and hat and left the pub. Jim turned right towards Bashall Eaves and began to walk at his usual brisk pace along the deserted Clitheroe road.

Back at Bashall Hall, Polly and Lily were expecting him and had his supper ready and prepared for when he got home. Albert Pickles was getting ready for bed, and turned in at 9 o'clock. Lily Lee followed suit a few minutes later. Jack Lee was by now deep in his shorthand study in The Prayer Room, just off the living room where Polly had built a crackling fire for him.

---

* Harry Frankland's statement said that he never left his farm all day because it was the lambing season. I did not come across George Towler's statement.

** The list of those present is compiled from the statement given by the licensee Jack Barnes and various other police statements and should not, therefore, be taken as absolutely definitive.

† Unsubstantiated local rumours persist that a quarrel involving a woman took place during the course of the evening.

The Brieryforth gate and the Lurking Figure

Eager to get home on such a wild night, Jim put his head down and walked quickly along the dark road with the wind whistling and the rain lashing down. When he got 150 yards or so away from the Brieryforth gate, Jim saw the headlights of two cars heading towards him. Illuminated briefly in their headlights he saw a man standing in the road by the Brieryforth gate*, which was on the left hand side of the road, just opposite the entrance to Back Lane – the lane Jim needed to take to get home.

Jim caught only a brief a glimpse of the man, and told the police later that he did not recognise or speak to him. It is difficult to see how he could have done either of those things when he had only spotted this man for a split second from a hundred yards or so away, on a dark and wet night.

In the back seat of one of the cars whose headlamps apparently lit up the skulking figure sat Jim's farmhand, Tommy Kenyon. He had met up with some friends at the Red Pump and left with them at about 9.10 p.m. Tommy was in the car with four other people – Thomas Parker Allan from Accrington and his fiancée Miss Ashworth, (who were apparently unknown to Kenyon before that night), along with Billy Wright and Frank Ireland of Bashall Eaves. Parker Allan stated later that they passed the spot where Jim Dawson was shot at 9.15 p.m. and that they slowed down at the Brieryforth gate to drop Kenyon off. Tommy Kenyon then apparently changed his mind and decided to go on to the Swan and Royal Hotel in Clitheroe with the others. I have been unable to establish the identity of the occupants of the second car seen by Jim that night.

---

*The Brieryforth (pronounced Brid-i-ford) gate was so-named because it provided access to the track to Brieryforth Farm, which has now disappeared. In 1934, Tommy Simpson's son Cyril lived here.

Jim Dawson is placed on the Clitheroe Road by one witness, but unfortunately, the timing and location of this particular sighting are both unclear. Ernest Hodgson, a bus driver of Waterloo Buildings, Slaidburn, was on a bus travelling along the Bashall Eaves road between Slaidburn and Clitheroe at about 9 p.m. He was in the front and had a clear view of the road by the lights of the bus. According to his statement, about 200 yards on the Clitheroe side of Back Lane, opposite the Brieryforth gate (this is actually inaccurate as the entrance to Back Lane is opposite the Brieryforth gate) he saw Jim walking towards the bus and remarked, *"There's Jim going home!"* Why Ernest should feel he had to announce this fact to the other occupants of the bus is a bit of a puzzle.

Be that as it may, he saw nobody else on the road. Ernest Hodgson's testimony is valuable in that it places Jim walking towards home on the Clitheroe Road at some time shortly after 9.00 p.m. It has been suggested that Jim's version of his actions between leaving the Edisford Bridge and arriving home may have been a fabrication. But as we will see there was little time for Jim to have done anything other than walk home.

The Shooting

If Jim was telling the truth about his own murder, what happened in the next couple of minutes was witnessed only by Jim Dawson himself and the person (or persons) who attacked him.

Jim Dawson arrived at the Brieryforth gate. It was now about 9.15 p.m. By this time, there was no sign of anyone else around. The lurking figure Jim had briefly spotted from 150 yards down the road had melted away into the darkness. Jim left the Clitheroe road and turned right, into the narrow Back Lane, its high hedges on either side creating an impenetrably dark tunnel ahead of him.

Jim had walked 30 yards along the lane when he heard a strange noise behind him, which he later described as a 'click'. Almost immediately after hearing the sound, Jim felt a sharp stinging pain in his right shoulder. Thinking it was some sort of joke (we will hear more of these so-called 'jokes') and that somebody had pitched a stone at him, he did not even turn round. He shrugged the incident off, and continued to walk along the deserted lane. Jim Dawson arrived home at Bashall Hall at 9.20 p.m.

By this time Albert Pickles and Lily Lee had already gone to bed and the only people still up and about were Polly Pickles and Jack Lee. Tommy Kenyon was still out.

Jack Lee remembers the night of the shooting well. Having finished his shorthand study, Jack went through the stair hall into the kitchen. Jim said to him, *"Oh, I thought you had gone to bed."* Jack remembers that Jim had hung up his overcoat and was sitting at the kitchen table awaiting his supper, which Polly duly placed in front of him. She had prepared cold roast pork with apple sauce. Jack comments that he always found it rather odd that Jim had a main meal so late at night. The rest of the family ate much earlier in the evening.

The Brieryforth gate taken from Back Lane, 2003. It was by this gate that Jim Dawson saw a lurking figure as he walked home from Edisford on the night of the shooting. *Photo: author*

Inset: Back Lane (sometimes known as the narrow lane) taken from the Brieryforth gate in 2003. After walking some thirty yards up this lane, Jim Dawson was shot in the back on the night of March 18, 1934. *Photo: author*

Jim ate a hearty supper, after which he sat in the chair by the kitchen fire for about ten minutes. Not one word did he utter regarding the attack. His behaviour and demeanour seemed perfectly normal, and neither Jack nor Polly noticed anything at all amiss. But at 9.40 p.m., much to their surprise he took off his jacket, hung it on the back of his chair and announced that he was going to bed. This was unusual behaviour as Jim never normally went to bed without giving Albert Pickles and Tommy Kenyon their work schedule for the farm for the following day.

The Long Night

Jim then took himself off upstairs, still without any mention of what had happened to him in Back Lane only half an hour before. It is likely that after Jim had eaten his supper, the physical and mental shock of what had happened finally hit him. Up until that point the four beers and gin he had imbibed at the pub may have had a mild anaesthetising effect.

After another half hour or so at 10.20 p.m., Jack Lee also called it a night. Holding a candle to light his way, he climbed the stairs to the bedroom on the second floor which he shared with his Uncle Jim. As Jack was getting ready for bed, Jim said to him, *"Are they all in?"* referring to Albert Pickles and Tommy Kenyon. (Jim did not seem to realise that Albert had stayed in that night, and had already gone to bed.) At that point Jack heard Tommy Kenyon coming in, and could answer his uncle in the affirmative - yes, everyone was now in the house. Tommy Kenyon's original statement to the police confirms this information. He told them that he left the Swan and Royal Hotel in Clitheroe at 10 o'clock and returned home at 10.30 p.m., by which time everyone else had gone to bed.

Jim Dawson was in for a long and miserable night. Jack Lee woke up several times during the night, in spite of being a relatively heavy sleeper, and heard the sound of his uncle moving around restlessly in bed, tossing this way and that. For by midnight Jim found himself in extreme discomfort.

He said in his statement to the police, *"After I had been in bed a couple of hours I found that my right arm was stiff, and pained so when I moved, and I felt that it had been bleeding. I then realised that I had been shot and I thought that the man I had seen standing at Brieryforth gate was responsible for the wound. I did not think the wound was serious, as it had stopped bleeding, so I did not rouse the household."* Jim went on, *"I did not get to sleep again, it pained me when I moved. In fact I could not get out of bed."*

To anyone outside the family, Jim's behaviour in retiring to bed without mentioning the attack and refusing to rouse the household in spite of being in extreme pain must seem bizarre. Indeed, it is one of the aspects of the case which has caused intense speculation in the media. But as his sister Lily Lee said, *"Anyone knowing him will understand why he would say nothing. He was of a very reserved nature and rarely told if he was ill."*

This behaviour also strikes a familiar chord personally, because my father, Jack Lee, has always acted in a very similar manner. When I was living at home I remember that if Jack was feeling ill or out of sorts he took himself off to bed without a word to anyone (including his wife, Olive).

"*Where's dad?*" my sister Patricia or I would ask, realising he had disappeared. "*He's gone to bed,*" my mother would reply in a worried fashion. "*I don't think he can be feeling very well.*"

Whether this is a peculiar family trait, or merely a trait common amongst Yorkshire men I do not know. But I feel sure that, if put in the same situation, Jack Lee would have behaved and reacted in exactly the same way as his uncle Jim Dawson on the night he was shot.

The Next Morning

By the morning of Monday, March 19th, even Jim could not ignore the situation any longer. He waited for Lily Lee to come into the bedroom as usual to wake her son Jack at 7.40 a.m. It must have been an immense relief when he finally heard her footsteps approaching and the bedroom door opening, as it meant that awful night was finally over with. However stoical he may have seemed on the outside, Jim must surely have lain there the whole night turning over in his mind what had happened and praying that he hadn't sustained a really serious injury. What he must have gone through, both mentally and physically in the long, dark and lonely hours of that Sunday night does not bear thinking about.

Jack remembers clearly what happened next. "*My mother came to waken me and when she came into the room my uncle asked her to look at his back.*"

Lily duly examined Jim's back and saw a large wound in his shoulder. Horrified, she exclaimed, "*Oh, Jim, whatever is the matter?*" Jim's back and bedclothes were soaking in blood.

He replied, "*I think somebody must have shot at me last night.*"

Lily exclaimed, "*Why didn't you tell us?*"

Jim explained, "*I didn't think anything about it. I thought I had been hit by a stone. I saw a man stood at the bottom of the lane and when I was about 25 yards up the lane, heard a click and at the same time felt a stone in my back.*"

Jack Lee remembers that there was also a substantial pool of blood under the bed, where it had seeped right through the mattress. He quickly jumped out of bed. "*I thereupon got dressed swiftly and dashed downstairs to ascertain why I hadn't seen anything amiss the night before. His jacket was hung up in the kitchen and on looking at the back of the jacket I was unable to see any damage, but on feeling the cloth I at last found a slit - cunningly hidden by the weave and colour. I then took down his overcoat (mac) and immediately there was a definite*

Elizabeth Hannah Dawson (Lily), Jim's sister (my grandmother), circa 1904. *Photo: family archive*

Jim's older sister, Mary (Polly) Dawson, circa 1906. *Photo: family archive*

slit to be seen. Obviously no-one had seen this when he came in as he followed his usual course of taking it off as he came in. An astonishing fact (to me) was that there was no trace of blood on the inside or outside of both garments. I then set off for Blackburn to Guests Business College and never saw Uncle Jim alive again."

What Jack had not noticed (but his mother did) was that there were three tiny drops of blood at the top of the stairs. Jim's wound had obviously started to bleed slightly even before he had reached his bedroom.

While Jack Lee was busy playing amateur detective, his mother Lily had taken the opportunity to call Polly into Jim's bedroom. Polly was amazed that Jim did not appear to be particularly worried by his condition. He sat up in bed for a while, drinking a cup of tea and smoking his pipe. No doubt after a great deal of sisterly nagging common sense finally prevailed, for Jim eventually agreed that the doctor and police should be called out. We have already mentioned that there was no telephone at Bashall Hall, and it was therefore necessary to go next door to use the telephone belonging to the Ormerod family at Bashall Hall cottage.

Dr. John Cooper of 3-5 Railway View and The Text House, Clitheroe, was the family doctor who arrived at 10 o'clock. He had not treated Jim for any illness for over seven years and his initial opinion on examining the wound was that Jim had not been shot. However, he suggested Jim should have an X-ray examination as a precaution *"because it would be a good idea to see if there was anything in there."*

Meanwhile, the police had also been informed of the previous night's incident, and P.C. Sheldon arrived from Waddington on his bicycle to take a statement. (Presumably this was the best that could be done for 'fast response' in 1934.) All the clothing Jim had worn the night before was handed over as evidence to the police constable.

A little later on, after the police and doctor had gone, the family gathered in the kitchen to discuss the situation. Tommy Kenyon, the farmhand, joined them and said to Jim, *"What have you been doing?"* (In other words, what on earth is going on?) Jim's reply is interesting. He told Tommy Kenyon that he had seen a man in the road, and felt a sting in his back. He commented that he thought it was a catapult shot caused by a stone or sod (of earth). Tommy Kenyon then posed a very sensible and pertinent question - why had he not turned round and confronted his assailant?

Jim's answer to that was simple. *"I didn't want another one."*

"It looked like a Dum-Dum bullet"

Lily decided to accompany her brother to Blackburn for his X-ray examination. She needed to go into Blackburn that day in any case to visit Guests Business College, probably to settle the bill for her son Jack's college fees. Their sister Annie, who had been away, was still in ignorance of the previous evening's dramatic events. Jim and Lily took a taxi to her place of employment (as housekeeper to a grocer called Hargreaves in Clitheroe) and apprised her of the situation. They then continued by taxi to Blackburn.

Rather than attend The Blackburn and East Lancashire Royal Infirmary, Jim chose (or was advised by the police) to have his examination carried out by a private radiologist, Dr. Frederick William Taylor, J.P., M.D., at 51 Preston New Road. The results of the X-ray must have shocked Jim and Lily to the core, as it revealed an object 'like a bird's egg' lodged in Jim's right side under his arm. Lily Lee said later that it looked like a dum-dum[*] bullet. If he was still thinking that the previous night's attack was some sort of joke or prank, the sight of that bullet must have caused him to think again. Dr. Taylor's recommendation was that he have an operation to remove it immediately. Jim refused, and went home.

What on earth can have possessed Jim Dawson take such a dangerous and irresponsible course of action? There could be several reasons. It could have been the cost of the operation, or possibly fear of the operation itself. He may well have thought that undergoing surgery was potentially more risky than leaving well alone. As a war veteran, Jim knew that many soldiers shot in the war were still walking around with bullets inside them without suffering any ill effects. Indeed one of Jack Lee's uncles, Captain Bert Lee, walked around with a bullet from the Great War inside his body for some time. Much to Bert Lee's (not to mention everybody else's) astonishment, the bullet suddenly popped out through the roof of his mouth nine years after he had been shot, leaving no sign of an exit wound whatsoever.

Jack has his own views concerning why Jim refused the operation on Monday, 19th March. He says, *"Much was made in the television programme 'The Village That Wouldn't Talk' of Jim insisting on returning to the farm but this was in order to give Albert and Tommy Kenyon instruction for the day, which he would normally have done the night before."*

It hardly seems sensible to delay a life-saving operation in order to tell subordinates what to do. However, we are talking with the benefit of hindsight, of course, and Jim had no inkling at this point that the bullet lodged in his armpit would eventually kill him.

Superintendent Elliott of Settle

Jim Dawson, then, returned to Bashall Hall on Monday afternoon with the bullet still firmly lodged in his shoulder. Later on that afternoon, Superintendent Elliott of the West Riding Police travelled from Settle to interview Jim at Bashall Hall. It has often been asserted that the officers investigating the case were 'strangers from the other side of the Pennines'. In Elliott's case at least this is completely untrue. He was quite familiar with the area and indeed had recently investigated poaching offences in the Forest of Bowland. However, murder was a different matter and Elliott had no idea of what was

---

[*] These were large British military bullets originally produced as an experiment at the Dum Dum Arsenal in India. They were .303 calibre, with the jacket nose open to expose the lead core. These bullets were outlawed for use in warfare by the Hague Convention in 1899. During the Great War, the German Kaiser accused the Belgian government of having used dum dum bullets in battle, a charge strongly denied by the Belgians.

Main Photo:
Jim's brother Charles Henry Dawson (Harry) looking very dapper circa 1910.
Photo: family archive

Inset:
Harry Dawson in about 1960 at his retirement bungalow at Waddington which he built himself.
Photo: J. G. Lee

in store for either himself, or his team of detectives, in the deceptively sleepy community of Bashall Eaves during the next few months. At this point, the incident seemed to be a relatively routine case of malicious wounding. Little did Elliott realise that he was about to initiate enquires into one of the most famous and mysterious crimes of the twentieth century.

Superintendent Elliott arrived at Bashall Hall at 4.15 p.m. Jim must have been mobile and reasonably alert at this point, as he was able to accompany the police officer down to the Brieryforth gate. He pointed out to him where the lurking figure had been standing and the place in Back Lane where he had heard the click, and felt the pain in his shoulder.

What Jim Dawson was actually doing, of course, (although neither man realised it at the time) was conducting a bizarre tour of the scene of his own murder. There can be few murder victims (if any) who have had the opportunity to describe the scene of their own murder to the investigating officer.

Elliott got to work. He ordered a wide search in the neighbourhood for cartridge and wad, and at this stage found nothing. Fields, hedgerows and ponds in the area were searched for possible clues. The police also took exact measurements from the Brieryforth gate to the point where Jim was shot and found it to be exactly 30 yards.

As Elliott and his team began their enquiries, Jim rested up at Bashall Hall. There was still the farm to think about, however, and new arrangements had to be made in order to keep the work ticking over. Harold Newhouse, aged 15, of nearby Vicarage Farm was taken on at Bashall Hall Farm to lend a hand with the farm work while Jim was incapacitated. Nominally, Albert Pickles took over Jim's role in overall charge of the farm, (though Jim's brother, Harry Dawson was to supervise him) which left Tommy Kenyon free to do the work normally carried out by Albert.

It is to young Harold Newhouse's statement that we owe most of our knowledge of the events of the next day. Harold arrived at Bashall Hall at 7 a.m. on Tuesday 20th March, and joined the household for breakfast. While Jim lay upstairs in bed, everybody discussed the shooting. Lily and Polly repeatedly said that '*it was a bad job*' and hoped the police would soon track down the culprit. Later on at dinner time, Harry Dawson arrived from Waddington and Jim struggled downstairs where Harry gave him a shave. Harry pleaded with his injured brother to tell the police all he knew.

The Death of Jim Dawson

It was becoming evident that Jim's condition was rapidly worsening, and Dr. Cooper was again sent for. His examination revealed that the wound was not looking as healthy as it had done, and was becoming infected. In the days before antibiotics, this was very serious news indeed.

It was decided (probably by Harry Dawson, who without doubt took complete charge of the situation as soon as he arrived) that Jim should be taken to a private nursing home at 20 Shear Bank Road, Blackburn. This establishment was run by a Miss J. Milligan, sister-in-charge, and here Jim would receive the specialised nursing attention he evidently required. Just before he left home he said to Albert Pickles, *"Be careful and look after the sheep while I'm away."* By tea-time (about 5 o'clock) Jim had left Bashall Hall, never to return there alive. He was operated upon later that same day in the nursing home and the enormous bullet was at last removed from his armpit.

The evening following Jim's departure from Bashall Hall must have been a sombre occasion indeed. All conversation revolved around the shooting. Over and over again during the course of the evening Lily and Polly said that *"they hoped it would be found out who had done it, as they could not think he had enemies or know of any person who would want to do him harm"*. Tommy Kenyon was quick to echo the sisters' sentiments, but Albert Pickles and Jack Lee (who had by that evening rejoined the household having stayed elsewhere the previous night) seemed to have little to say on the matter. Albert was probably feeling somewhat overpowered at having to step into his Uncle Jim's shoes, while Jack, at 17 years old, possibly did not appreciate the seriousness of the situation. He also had other things on his mind, including a new job he was soon to take up. It may also be said that neither of them was particularly fond of their uncle, who was always more popular with women than he was with men. Once or twice, the adult conversation turned briefly to farming, but the sisters could concentrate on little else but their brother's plight.

On Wednesday, 21st March, the Manchester Guardian reported the shooting of Jim Dawson as an incident of wounding. While Jim lay deteriorating rapidly in the Blackburn nursing home, Lily, Polly and Annie waited anxiously at home for news of his condition. They were informed that Jim was as well as could be expected. In addition to worrying about their brother, the sisters had to deal with the police, who arrived to take statements from all those resident at Bashall Hall. Harold Newhouse commented in his statement (taken at a later date) that he remembered some person (he does not specify whom) saying that they thought Jim had not told the police all he knew and that he was hiding something.

The fateful day of Thursday, 22nd March brought the news that Jim Dawson's condition was causing extreme concern. While obviously very poorly indeed, he evidently had no idea just how ill he really was, as is made clear by the following excerpt from the Inquest Report *(from the Clitheroe Advertiser and Times, 29 June, 1934)*.

> George Leach, assistant clerk to the Blackburn Magistrates, said that on Thursday March 22nd, he went to the Nursing Home in Shear Bank Road, Blackburn, to take a statement from James Dawson.
>
> The Coroner: You took his dying depositions?
>
> Leach: **He did not think he was dying.**
>
> The Coroner: What was the statement?
>
> Leach: Mr Dawson said, "I declare I do not know who fired the shot. There is nothing else I can tell you that I know of."

That afternoon, a police officer arrived at Bashall Hall with the terrible news that Jim did not have long to live, and the family rushed to his bedside. Jim Dawson, a reserved Yorkshire farmer supposedly without an enemy in the world, died with his family around him at approximately 3.30 p.m.

It was now a case of murder.

CHAPTER 5

No Development, No Clue, No Motive

The Murder Investigation

JIM'S unexpected and peculiar death threw the Dawson family into a state of shock. While his brothers and sisters struggled to maintain some semblance of normality and carry on as best they could with their everyday activities, the murder marked the beginning of a period of continuous strain, not only for the residents of Bashall Hall but for the entire Bashall Eaves community.

Practically every person in the neighbourhood had already been interviewed regarding Jim's wounding, without any result. However, when he died as a result of the attack, the entire atmosphere of the enquiry changed in the wink of an eye. The officers of the West Riding Constabulary shifted into high gear as they launched an all-out murder investigation. By this time, of course, the killer had already gained four days' grace in which to dispose of the weapon and arrange a suitable alibi.

The Murder Investigation Begins

On the night Jim died at the Blackburn nursing home, Superintendent Elliott and other detectives interviewed William Reid Chew at the Model Lodging House in Clitheroe for over two hours, until 2 a.m. on the following Friday morning. Chew was taken in for immediate interrogation because he had recently been sacked from his job at Bashall Town by Tommy Simpson. We have already described how he had been heard to make disparaging remarks about the farm while travelling on a bus, which was overheard by Jim Dawson's sister Annie, and repeated to the Simpsons. The police thought Chew may therefore have attacked Jim in revenge for having lost his job, but this line of enquiry was soon dropped. At 3 a.m. the police departed from Clitheroe to pursue their enquiries elsewhere.

On Friday, 23rd March the post-mortem examination of Jim Dawson's body was carried out at Blackburn Police Mortuary by the police surgeon, Dr. G. Bailey. He pronounced the cause of death to be septicaemia, set up from the wound in the shoulder. In the light of speculation and inaccuracies which have arisen over the past 70 years regarding the trajectory of the bullet wound, the post-mortem report is here reproduced verbatim for the first time. It does not, of course, make pleasant reading.

REPORT

on the Post-mortem examination

of the body of JAMES DAWSON,

aged 46, of Bashall Hall,

made at Blackburn Police Mortuary

on Friday, March 23rd 1934

by Dr C. Bailey, Police Surgeon, Blackburn.

EXTERNAL EXAMINATION

Development:
Very well developed and muscular. Height: 5 ft 5 inches.

Nourishment:
Well nourished.

Signs of recent violence:
There was a wound on the back of the right shoulder just below the spine of the right scapula. This wound was nearly horizontal and had been made to open up a bullet wound which could be seen in the depths of the skin opening towards its outer angle. The bullet wound in the muscle was less than half an inch diameter and the tissues surrounding it were softened by suppuration. The direction of the wound which was 4 feet 4 inches above the right heel was nearly exactly horizontal from behind forwards and penetrated the scapula forming an opening through which the gloved fingers could be passed. The track ended in the axilla between the muscular layer covering the front surface of the scapula and the chest wall. In this situation there was pus. The ribs were uninjured.

There was a large surgical drainage incision 5 inches long running horizontally from the lower angle of the scapula forwards and ending on the upper part of the upper arm.

INTERNAL EXAMINATION

Thorax

The lungs and heart were normal. The intima (inner surface of the aorta) was of a deep red colour due to putrefaction.

Abdomen

The kidneys were small and granular with little kidney substance and much pelvic fat - chronic nephritis. The spleen was small and of normal appearance.

Head

The superficial vessels of the brain were congested.

Cause of Death

Death from septicaemia resulting from a gunshot wound in the right shoulder.

R. L. Sutherland, 24th March 1934

It should be noted once and for all that the bullet entered Jim's body almost exactly horizontally, and not at an angle, as has been asserted on several occasions.

It is interesting to note that septicaemia generally occurs in people whose resistance to infection is already low, or being overtaxed. Those with kidney trouble are considered particularly at risk, and we have already seen that Jim was suffering from a kidney complaint. It is possible, therefore, that had Jim been in better health generally, he might have recovered from the gunshot wound.

On Saturday 24th March the Blackburn Coroner, Mr. T. R. Thompson, opened the Inquest. The proceedings were formal and lasted only three minutes. Polly Pickles gave evidence of identification, and a Clitheroe gunsmith was questioned as to the effective range of this particular bullet if fired from a revolver. He said that 35 yards would be a long range for the bullet to penetrate. Also attending the Inquest were Superintendent Elliott of Settle, and Chief Superintendent Wilfred Blacker, head of the West Riding C.I.D. at Wakefield.

The West Riding Constabulary was unusual in that it boasted a functioning Criminal Investigation Department at this time. This was in marked contrast to other police forces. Indeed the lack of detective training and absence of C.I.D. units had become such a serious problem that in 1934 the Home Secretary appointed a committee to look into the whole matter. In the West Riding, however, detectives received a three week training course. This was, unfortunately, to prove woefully inadequate for a case of such complexity.

Wilfred Blacker had been placed in overall charge of Jim Dawson's case by the Chief Constable, Colonel Frank Brook. According to Yorkshire Television's 1979 documentary "The Village That Wouldn't Talk", Wilf Blacker was something special. He was described as a man who had one foot in the Victorian times but also knew the value of forensic science in the investigation of murder. *"He came to Bashall Eaves fresh from a triumph in York where he'd solved a murder, probably thinking, 'I won't be long with this one!'"* Watching the local gunsmith giving evidence, Blacker decided that this wouldn't do at all. He required a top forensic ballistics expert on this case. He therefore went right to the top and called in the famous London gun expert, Robert Churchill.

The Gun Expert

Robert Churchill had joined the family firm, E. J. Churchill (Gun Makers) in 1891. By 1934, the company (still trading) had the honour of being gunsmith to H.R.H. the Prince of Wales, and Robert Churchill himself had been an eminent ballistics expert for several years. He was a regular lecturer at the Police College at Hendon, and in 1934 sat on the committee to consider the new Firearms Act. *"Then,"* says his biographer Macdonald Hastings, *"at the peak of his career, when none doubted his opinion, he was involved in a case which utterly defeated him."*

The case was, of course, that of the shooting of Jim Dawson.

Not being blessed with the gift of foresight he delved into the case with gusto, and with, no doubt, the same high level of confidence as Chief Superintendent Blacker. According to Macdonald Hastings' BBC drama-documentary "Call the Gun Expert: The Perfect Crime" (1964), Blacker sent the bullet and other forensic evidence down to London for Churchill to examine.

His opinion was that the bullet had been home-made for a specific purpose, or weapon, because it had been cut from a steel rod and trimmed and filed to size by hand. (He also suggested that it could have been a reduced ball bearing.) The tools required to fashion such a bullet were a workbench, a vice and two files. As Churchill pointed out, any workshop or garage would have been equipped to manufacture it, as would any reasonably well-organised farm.

Churchill commented that he would normally expect the gun barrel to produce characteristic markings on the bullet after it had been fired, but in this case the reverse was true. Because the bullet was of hard steel, it would have marked the barrel of the gun which fired it rather than the other way round. Find the gun, he said, and he would be able to match it up with the markings on the bullet.

The gun expert then considered the possible murder weapon. The bullet was too large, he decided, to have been fired from an ordinary service revolver. It could have been fired from a shotgun if wrapped in paper - but why go to the trouble of making a bullet when ordinary ammunition was so readily available? Churchill was of the opinion that the bullet must have been made specially to use in an obsolete firearm, for example a muzzle-loading pistol, many of which had a half-inch bore.

Armed with Robert Churchill's information, Superintendent Elliott and his team combed the Bashall Eaves district for files, lengths of steel rod and any implements which could cut steel. They did not, it seems, conduct their search in a particularly efficient fashion at times. On one occasion, Jack Lee and Albert Pickles were chatting in The Chill Room at Bashall Hall when two policemen prowled in. The two young men watched in fascination as the detectives peered around carefully. After a couple of minutes Albert became bored. *"What are you looking for exactly?"* he enquired.

"Anything which will cut steel," replied one of the officers.

"What do you think that is, then?" said Albert, pointing to a hack-saw hanging up on the wall in full view.

"DOH!" (or whatever the 1930s equivalent might have been), exclaimed the detective. Presumably these particular officers needed to consult their 'Ladybird Book of How to Search Buildings Properly' again.

As well as searching for files and lengths of steel rod, everyone's farm machinery was also scrutinised. This was probably due to Tommy Kenyon's suggestion that the bullet looked as if it may have been cut from a raking machine or something similar. The police also collected all the guns from every farm throughout the Bowland and Clitheroe area. These were temporarily confiscated for examination for barrel scratches. The owners of the weapons were required to give a written statement describing their movements on the night of 18th March and to provide exact details of household members, and the names of anyone else working on the farms on the night in question. The farmers and their families never forgot these police visits. Mary Frankland of Edisford Hall Farm said in 1980, when she was 75 years old, that she remembered as if it were yesterday the moment the police came to search their property, and how every one of their collection of old guns was taken in for examination.

According to the Clitheroe Advertiser and Times on March 30th, *"It is literally true to say that not a stone has been left unturned in the effort to solve this baffling mystery."* But in spite of the best efforts of Chief Superintendent Blacker and his team, day followed day with the same report, *"No development, no clue, no motive"*.

Jim Dawson's Funeral

The murdered man's funeral was held on Monday 26th March. The vicar of Mitton, the Reverend J. Robinson, held a brief service for the family at Bashall Hall. A second service then took place in the church.

Many of the friends Jim Dawson had made in the business and poultry world joined the family, as did representatives from the Bashall Eaves and Browsholme Agricultural Show Committee. Lady Worsley-Taylor and Sir John Worsley-Taylor, the owners of the Bashall Hall estate, sent their agent Mr. Airey to represent them.

After the service Jim's coffin was carried solemnly to the family grave in the churchyard by his friends Tommy Simpson of Bashall Town, Bill Eccles of Browsholme, Harry Frankland of Edisford Hall Farm and George Towler of Edisford Bridge Farm.

Jim was buried with John, his brother, who had been interred only eleven months earlier. As the family watched the coffin being lowered into the earth, Polly said to her brother Harry, *"Jim's gone with a secret and I believe we shall never find out what it is. He has taken it with him"* It is difficult to shake off the notion that Jim Dawson's murderer may well have attended his funeral and mingled with the genuine mourners.

The grave of Jim Dawson in Mitton graveyard. *Photo: J. G. Lee*

On the following day (March 24th), several hundred members of the local farming community stood in silence at Clitheroe Auction Mart as tributes were paid to Jim's memory. Mr E. Whitehead, Chairman of Directors, said that it was fitting that the farmers of the district should put on record their appreciation of the character of Mr. Dawson, whose death occurred so mysteriously and tragically.

As the farmers paid their respects, the police issued a broadcast appealing for help, which ran thus:

"About 9.15 on Sunday March 18 on the road at Bashall Eaves, near Clitheroe, a man was shot in the back and has since died. The bullet was of steel and had the appearance of being home-made. The police desire to interview any person who may have been in the vicinity and specially request the following people to come forward.

1. A broadly-built man carrying a walking stick.

2. A man and a woman who had with them a dog.

3. A young man wearing an overcoat and trilby hat, in company with a woman wearing a green coat.

4. A fairly tall man, wearing brown overcoat and trilby.

Any person who may be able to [give] any information should communicate at once with the Chief Constable of the West Riding Constabulary, Wakefield, telephone number Wakefield 3194."

As well as the people mentioned above, the police were anxious to trace a man who had been riding a bicycle along the Bashall Road some distance behind Jim Dawson when he left the Edisford Bridge Hotel.

Red Herrings

Throughout this first week, strange incidents were reported to the police, whose resources must have been stretched to the limit. By far the most bizarre story of all was told to the police by Mr. Leslie Harrison of Grimshaw Street, Clitheroe. He described how on Tuesday afternoon at 4.15 p.m., as he was walking along the road from Edisford Bridge towards Bashall Eaves, he was overtaken by a man. The man was smartly dressed in a brown striped suit, white shirt and chocolate tie. On his head he wore a brown trilby hat, turned down all round and without a band. In other words, he appears to have been dressed up like a gangster. The man had a fresh complexion and had a thin-featured face.

As the man caught up with him, Harrison said, *"It is a bad do about yon farmer being shot and not knowing who has done it."*

The man replied, *"Aye, it is getting more like New York every day."* After a pause he added, *"They might think I had done it if they saw this,"* and at the same time he pulled a gun from his right hand jacket pocket. Harrison said that it was quite a small gun, but it was certainly no toy. Having presumably caused Leslie Harrison to jump out of his skin in alarm, the man left him and followed the footpath across Thirty Acre Field in the direction of Higher Hodder.

We hear no more about the Al Capone of Bashall Eaves. Presumably this strange man was merely an addict of gangster movies such as 'Public Enemy' rather than a dangerous lunatic (although he could have been both, of course).

Residents of the district were quite understandably now reporting anything in the least out of the ordinary. On 30th March, for example, the police were called out to Mitton, where Mrs. Carter of Brick House reported a man acting strangely. Seeing he was being watched, this man took off at a run into a nearby wood. The wood was searched thoroughly, but no sign was found of any man. It is hardly surprising that the local people were feeling insecure with a killer on the loose.

Tommy Simpson and the Smuggled Gun

While the police were busy chasing fruitlessly around in Mitton Wood, Tommy Simpson of Bashall Town was about to do something very, very stupid indeed. The action he was about to take was to have far-reaching repercussions.

As we have already mentioned, one of Simpson's farm workers (who was also his nephew) was called Henry Bleazard, and Henry lived at Bashall Town with the Simpson family. He had in his possession a .22 rifle, the existence of which he wished to conceal from the police. Henry confided to his Uncle Tommy that he was scared about the gun being at the farm. Tommy Simpson, for reasons best known to himself, agreed to smuggle the gun out of Bashall Town and to hide it with relatives in Billington, near Whalley. He removed the gun to this location on either 30th or 31st March.

Albert Pickles (left) and friend dipping sheep in Bashall Brook, 1934.
Photo: family archive

Tommy Simpson's farmhand and nephew Henry Bleazard (left) with friend Jim Lambert about to take a dip in Bashall Brook, 1934.
Photo: family archive

Meanwhile, the police investigation had entered its second week and saw ever increasing activity. Throughout the week, police officers continued their search of the fields and hedges in the immediate vicinity of Back Lane and also further afield. The Clitheroe Advertiser and Times tells us that during these searches at least one interesting item had come to light. What this was is not revealed to the public. It may well refer to what the police thought might be a breakthrough discovery at the Simpson farm.

For Henry Bleazard, not content with persuading his Uncle Tommy to smuggle his gun out for him, also attempted on 3rd April to smuggle out a box of cartridge filler by giving it to his mother, who took it to Billington. Not only this, but it had come to the attention of the police that Bleazard had been claiming that he had found out how to make silent cartridges and had even shown Albert Pickles the instructions.

It is not too difficult to work out how the police eventually discovered all this secret activity. They were keeping a close watch on the movements of every member of the Bashall Eaves farming community, and both Bashall Hall and Bashall Town were under 24-hour surveillance. Having clocked an unusual amount of coming and going between Bashall Town and Billington, the officers bided their time and then swooped.

At 2.40 p.m. on 6th April 1934, Tommy Simpson was present when the smuggled gun was handed over to the police by his relative in Billington. Superintendent Blacker must have been rubbing his hands in glee and thinking, *"This is it. We've cracked it!"* Why risk trying to get rid of a gun in the middle of a murder investigation unless the gun was the murder weapon they were seeking?

Why indeed, because we hear no more about it. It was yet another red herring. The barrel of Bleazard's gun cannot have carried the markings to match it up with the bullet that killed Jim Dawson. What had possessed Tommy Simpson to take the risky action of smuggling his nephew's gun away from his farm during a murder enquiry is anyone's guess. Possibly he suspected that the weapon might actually have been used in the murder, or alternatively the gun may have been used during other illicit activities in the neighbourhood or even have been stolen. Be that as it may, Tommy Simpson and Henry Bleazard must have assumed they were off the hook as neither of them was subsequently arrested in connection with Jim's murder.

However, the seeds of suspicion had been firmly sown regarding the Simpson family and their deeds. Baulked of their prey and not at all happy, (or even convinced of the Simpsons' innocence) the police continued to watch Bashall Town round the clock.

All this was most unfortunate, for we have seen that Tommy Simpson and Jim Dawson had been on very friendly terms all their lives, and Tommy visited Bashall Hall regularly, both before and after the murder took place. Mary Frankland of Edisford Hall Farm commented in 1980, *"Mrs. Simpson told my mother that Tommy Simpson was changed by the murder. He would be milking, turn round and see the police looking at him. They even went into his house and looked under all the carpets."* Jack Lee remembers that the police had Bashall Town completely surrounded for over two months. This state of affairs must have placed Tommy Simpson under almost unbearable stress.

Things were not improved for Simpson when, in answer to police enquiries, stories began to emerge about his son Cyril (of Brieryforth Farm) and Henry Bleazard carrying out secret poaching raids on neighbouring farms. Albert Pickles said that Jim Dawson knew all about this, and had advised Albert to keep away from Bleazard and Cyril Simpson. Jim had also said that he was going to inform the farmer concerned (a man rejoicing in the delightful name of Stout Marsden) what was going on and who was responsible for the losses. Another witness commented, without giving any reason, that *"Cyril Simpson was bitter against Jim Dawson."*

Cherchez La Femme

Detectives also began to gather information about Tommy Simpson's eldest daughter Nancy. Jack Lee remembers her only as *"a nice girl - very friendly and pleasant"*. He was probably too young to appreciate Nancy's other attributes. Nancy Simpson was 21 years old at the time and was a girl way ahead of her time. An exceptionally attractive and uninhibited young woman, according to some sources she would think nothing of

Jim's brother Robert Eastwood Dawson (Bob) circa 1912, who was convinced his brother's murder was because of a woman. Bob founded the present Dawson's Department Store.
Photo: family archive

stripping off in mixed company to bathe in Bashall Brook. While nobody would bat an eyelid today, this free and easy behaviour caused a few raised eyebrows (and other things) in the early 1930s. Needless to say, she was exceedingly popular with the local youths. Tommy Kenyon recalled in 1980 that, *"Nancy was only happy when she was with a lad. She were a fit lass, she were that"*. How other women reacted to her may be imagined. The comment, "Burn the witch!" springs readily to mind. Unfortunately, poor Nancy's luck ran out in 1931 when she had fallen pregnant and given birth to a son whom she named Jimmy.

We can almost hear the rather shrill tone in which one of Jim's sisters stated to the police in 1934, *"Nancy Simpson, 21, has loose morals and is very fond of men. My brother [Jim] used to speak to her and she usually spoke to him on sexual matters."*

The police appeared to be investigating the possibility that Jim was the father of Nancy's child, Jimmy Simpson, thus giving Tommy Simpson a motive for murdering Jim. But none of this would do. Nancy's child had been born a couple of years before the murder and for Tommy Simpson to wait two years to take revenge on his daughter's 'ravisher' was untenable as a motive. The father of the son Nancy bore in 1931 is known beyond reasonable doubt, and it was not Jim Dawson. This does not rule out, of course, the idea that Jim may have been enjoying some sort of liaison with Nancy in 1934. Local rumours to this effect were evidently abroad at the time, as Chief Superintendent Blacker despatched several officers to enquire into Jim's 'conduct with Nancy Simpson'.[*] The officers were presumably unimpressed with the information received and never succeeded in establishing a reasonable motive for murder within the Simpson household.

Nancy Simpson was by no means the only woman investigated by the West Riding Constabulary in connection with the murder. As soon as Jim died on 22nd March, the police began to look for a motive and the first statement taken concerning his love life is dated that very same night. The theory that the murder was a crime of passion was an active line of enquiry which was pursued for well over a month.

For a village that allegedly 'wouldn't talk', the residents of Bashall Eaves and Clitheroe were positively chatty when it came to pointing the police in the direction of women Jim had known over the years. The name Lily Barker comes up over and over again in the witness statements taken by the police and the lady in question was interviewed in Wales, along with her former landlords in Clitheroe and employers at the Higher Hodder public house. However, it could not be established from the police records whether or not her husband was ever interviewed. In any case, the line of enquiry appeared to go nowhere and we have to assume that the police pursued all the available leads until they reached a satisfactory conclusion.

Some family members, including his brother Bob, were also convinced that one of Jim Dawson's girlfriends would provide clues to the motive for his murder. Bob had abandoned the world of farming and was by this time working as a shop manager in Clitheroe.

---

[*] As a result of information laid by Jim Dawson's farmhand, Tommy Kenyon.

He gave a rather confusing statement to the police. In this statement we learn that Bob had accosted P.C. Brindle in Clitheroe, demanding to know why he had not been questioned about 'my brother's job'. On being told that the police probably thought he could not help them, Bob replied, *"I intend to help them even if they don't ask me. There is a woman at the back of this job."* Bob then asked if the Wrigleys (Lily Barker's landlords) had been interviewed and said, *"I am looking for a sharp featured man, the job is through jealousy. People will go to any length when they are jealous."*

A little later on that same day, Bob again accosted the policeman in Parson Lane in Clitheroe. P.C. Brindle advised him that the woman he had been asking about had moved to Wales. Bob replied to this, *"Well, I saw a man on the Railway Station at 6.40 p.m. on Wednesday last. I suspect him of doing the job...."He was reading a newspaper. He cringed when he saw me and put the paper under his jacket. I think he was reading the account of the murder."*

Bob described the man as being 5'9" tall, with a sallow complexion and sharp features. He also told the police constable that he intended to go round the public houses of Clitheroe that night with Nathan Sefton of Fox Street to see if they could find the man he had seen on the railway station and to obtain his name and address.

Whether or not the police followed up Bob's information could not be established from the case file. It is also difficult to place Bob's statement within the timescale of the police investigation as it bears the remarkable date of **"34th March 1934"**. Welcome to The Twilight Zone.

Jane Preston is another name which occurs frequently in the witness statements. But again, this line of enquiry seemed to fizzle out without result. The police officers went on to list every woman Jim had ever known, including those whom he had merely treated with a drink at local hostelries.

One entry on the list came as a bit of a shock. It read, *"A Belgian Woman from whom he was divorced 13 years ago."* It was only after following the enquiry through for a few weeks that it became apparent that the police seemed to be confusing the murder victim with another man called James Dawson. Jim Dawson's secret marriage and divorce would have been an interesting addition to the Dawson family records had it been true.

The Police Experiments – Shooting Sticks and Catapults

Back in Bashall Eaves, the atmosphere was charged with paranoia. Plain clothes men continued to hide behind bushes, mingled with local residents in the pubs and with the farmers at the Auction Mart asking about strangers, or merely listening in to conversations. Whenever a farmer who was engaged in his everyday tasks turned round, a detective hove into view. And, of course, a particularly close watch was being kept upon Jim Dawson's family at Bashall Hall. All the family's bank books and other financial paperwork were taken in for scrutiny. Police also continued their visits to local garages and forges seeking more information about home-made bullets.

Armed with information sent from London by Robert Churchill, the West Riding Constabulary began to carry out experiments using similar bullets to the one which killed Jim Dawson. Inspector Elliott managed to make one himself in five minutes flat. He tried placing it into a .410 cartridge and firing it from a rifle. To test its effect on human flesh the bullet was fired from a 30 yard range at a lump of meat in front of an oak timber. This resulted in the bullet passing straight through the piece of meat and embedding itself in the timber. Elliott therefore concluded that had the bullet been fired from such a weapon at such a range, it would have blown Jim's shoulder off as it passed straight through him.

He also discovered that had the bullet been fired from a 12 or 16 bore shotgun, the result would have been the same, as it would have been propelled a good 600 yards, passing through Jim's body at the 30 yard point.

Superintendent Elliott then considered the possibility of an air gun as the murder weapon. It was said at the Inquest, however, that the bullet would not fit into the barrel of an air gun. It only fitted into the barrel of an old-fashioned weapon known variously as an air cane, shooting stick and Poacher's Arm. According to Don Masters of E. J. Churchill, air canes were originally very expensive pieces of weaponry. A local farmer would not shell out the money for such a piece. The only people likely to own one would be the local gentry, who used them as self-defence against footpads while travelling about the countryside. When fully assembled, this weapon is about two feet long and can be readied for firing in advance using a foot pump. It is carried like a walking stick and indeed would be virtually indistinguishable from a walking stick[*] from a distance. Should trouble rear its ugly head, then all that was necessary was to point the shooting stick at the attacker, and fire. An air cane, then, looks nothing like a conventional gun and works by propelling the bullet on a charge of compressed air.

This weapon does not seem to have been considered as a serious candidate for the murder weapon at the time of the enquiry. When questioned at the Inquest, Superintendent Elliott commented that it was an old fashioned weapon, not one example of which came to light in their searches. Yet Jim Dawson's friend Bill Eccles remembers that shooting sticks were certainly still in use in the 1930s in the nearby Gisburn area. It is possible, therefore, that the police might have overlooked the dismantled parts of such a weapon and not recognised them for what they were. Why the police did not consider an air cane or similar weapon a little more seriously as the potential murder weapon is a bit of a mystery.

As well as being an out-of-date weapon, possibly a Poacher's Arm was ruled out because of the noise which Jim described having heard just before he was shot? This was, we will remember, a 'click' rather than the loud bang we would normally associate with a firearm.

---

* It is interesting to note that one of the potential witnesses whom the police asked to come forward and who failed to do so was *a broadly-built man carrying a walking stick*, who had been seen approaching the murder scene from the direction of Waddington.

It is worth mentioning that Jim would surely have recognised the sound of a gun being discharged as he had plenty of experience with firearms. The noise made by an air cane as it fires is not really a click - it is far louder than that, though less noisy, perhaps than a conventional gun.

One weapon, however, does make a definite click when it is fired but is more associated with schoolboy pranks than with murder. This weapon is a simple catapult. Superintendent Elliott took his home-made bullet and fired it from a catapult from a 30 yard range at its target, which was three thicknesses of cloth and 2 pieces of linen with a tin plate behind them. The cloth used was similar to that worn by Jim on the night he died. The bullet passed through the cloth and dented the tin plate thus producing an effect similar to that on the human victim. Moreover, the noise made by the catapult as it was fired was a most definite 'click'. The police were certainly not ruling out the possibility that the bullet had been fired from such an unconventional weapon.

However, by the end of the second week of the police investigation it was still the same old story. Still no clue. Still no motive. Nothing. As the third week commenced, the police officers concentrated yet again on the area around Bashall Hall and the murder scene around Back Lane. Several residents were closely questioned and buildings searched for the umpteenth time.

Albert and Jack – The Family Under Suspicion

My father, Jack Lee and more particularly his cousin Albert Pickles, seem to have moved into the role of prime suspects at this time. The police were suspicious of Jack and Albert because of their disagreement with Jim two weeks prior to the shooting and the two young men were repeatedly grilled over the coming weeks. Jack had recently left Guests Business College to start his first job as junior clerk in the office at Whalley Abattoir. He remembers the police officers turning up at his place of work to interview him. The manager of the abattoir, Jim Halliday, refused to allow the policemen to cart Jack off for interrogation as he was only 17 years old. He considered that an adult should be present during any such proceedings.

Be that as it may, Jack and Albert were eventually taken to Settle police station for interview at a later date. Jack recalls: *"Albert and I were taken to Settle Police Station for the Third Degree. The car in which we were taken reached speeds of 60 m.p.h. plus, and I expect the police thought that us country gobies would be so paralysed with fear on arrival that we would be easy meat. We thoroughly enjoyed the ride. The police also constantly used the ploy of 'good cop – bad cop' in interrogation, but I was quite amused by this as it appeared in several detective novels I had read – written by the famous author A.E.W. Mason."*

Albert and my father were vigorously questioned for a couple of hours in separate rooms as the police officers desperately tried to trick them into incriminating each other. Albert became extremely irritated and upset. He eventually lost his composure completely and began to swear at the questioning officers - never a good idea at the best of times, and this was scarcely the best of times - especially for an expert shot with both gun and catapult. In the light of the police experiments, it was natural that Albert would fall under extreme suspicion. Much of the questioning of the two cousins centred around Albert's movements on the night of the murder, and whether or not he could have left the house after he had ostensibly gone to bed at 9 o'clock.

Superintendent Blacker was always pretty convinced that the members of Jim's family knew more about the murder than they said, and he had particular doubts about Albert and his catapult. Eventually, however, the police grudgingly came to the conclusion that neither Albert nor Jack had any credible motive for wanting their uncle dead, and that it would have proved impossible for Albert to have left the house without alerting another member of the family.

Baulked of their prey yet again, the police were back to square one. And they were finding their enquiries in Bashall Eaves less and less comfortable as time went on. Things did not improve when some local village nitwits began to behave idiotically.

Jim's nephew Jack Lee relaxing on a strawing machine at Bashall Hall in 1933.
Photo: family archive

Albert Pickles, Jim's nephew, circa 1932.
Photo: family archive

The Practical Jokers

It is difficult to credit that in the middle of a murder enquiry, some people found it amusing to waste police time and resources by initiating a spate of 'practical jokes'. Whether or not these had any connection with April Fool's Day on 1st April is uncertain and I can find no record of any rural rituals specifically associated with the first two weeks of April. It is worth printing the newspaper report in full, as an illustration of the foolish behaviour with which the West Riding Constabulary had to contend in Bashall Eaves in April 1934, when they were attempting to solve the murder of a local resident:

"The police in unearthing a mass of detail at Bashall Eaves have discovered that the district has quite a reputation for its practical jokes. They have discovered, for instance, who painted a grey gelding until it resembled a zebra, and they have also obtained sundry hints as to who was responsible for certain white Wyandottes [a species of American fowl] *changing colour, one becoming green, another black, and a third scarlet, all in one night. They have also shrewd suspicions as to who removed a cartwheel from the neighbourhood of a local farm and trundled it a good mile before hurling it into a field. On the other hand, it is not clear who pushed the shafts of a cart through a locked gate and attached the horse at the other side. The police also know that a youth or gang of youths took the shot out of a cartridge, which they filled with corn, which was fired at the trousers of a man working in a stooping position in the middle of a field."*

(Clitheroe Advertiser and Times, April 13th 1934)

While a couple of these jokes seem harmless enough, (and, no, I am **not** referring to the painting of those defenceless animals), the crass insensitivity of these 'jokers' beggars belief. We really have to question the mentality of the people who considered it a lark to shoot at someone during a murder investigation. The West Riding police were having a difficult enough time as it was without being distracted by such stupidity on the part of local youths.

These incidents may also, of course, have planted the idea in Chief Superintendent Blacker's mind that it could have been an act of equally thoughtless stupidity on the part of a local which resulted in the death of Jim Dawson. Indeed, the subject was even raised by the Coroner at the Inquest on 25th June:

The Coroner: You know the natives of this district quite well. They go in for what we townspeople call full-blooded jokes.

P.C. Sheldon: Yes, they do.

The Coroner: Assuming one of these youths had been standing in this gateway and had a catapult with him. If he had seen the deceased walk past, would it be in keeping with their idea of a joke to have a shot at Dawson to see him jump?

P.C. Sheldon: It would.

These 'practical jokes' exasperated the police, and may also have been responsible for initiating the widely-held belief that the area was a rather backward and peculiar place.

The Shot Dog

Another bizarre incident which appeared in the pages of The Clitheroe Advertiser and Times on 13th April concerned the death of a local animal.

"Yesterday the police were interested in a dog at Bashall Hall. This animal was shot at some weeks ago and it is believed that a bullet struck the dog. X-ray photographs show that no such missile is lodging in the dog."

The dramatic implication was, of course, that the bullet had been removed and re-used. This brief comment in a local paper has been the cause of some speculation in recent years. Suggestions have been made that this animal may have been used for target practice by the murderer to test the efficiency of his home-made bullet. However, a quick perusal of the original X-ray examination report disposes of this idea once and for all.

F. W. TAYLOR, M.D.

Kirkside,
51 Preston New Road,
Blackburn
April 12 1934

X ray report of
   Mr. Dawson's dog
      Bashall Hall Farm

The radiograph shews 4 circular shadows which are obviously cast by metallic bodied - pellets. One lies a little distance below the tail at its junction with the body, another above the tail just below the skin close to the iliac bone. There are two others, one just below and a little above the ribs. The dark shadow running transversely is cast by gas in the intestine. There is no evidence of a larger metallic body.

Signed   F.W. Taylor, M.D.

As we can see, no large bullet had ever lodged in the body of this dog. Yet there is a strange angle to this story which the media never seems to have taken up (or were, perhaps unaware of). This is the fact that the dog which had been shot was Jim Dawson's own sheepdog, whose name was Shep. From the description of its injuries, it seems hardly likely that Jim would have put the dog down himself in such a manner. So the rather sinister question remains; who shot Jim Dawson's dog a couple of weeks before Jim himself was shot?

The Police Give Up

Nearly a month had now elapsed since the death of Jim Dawson, and the police were no nearer to catching his killer. There was still no whiff of any real motive and no genuine clue - merely an entire aquarium of red herrings swimming confusingly in and out of the picture. There was a vital clue missing and neither the police nor anyone else (apart from the person or persons who carried out the crime) knew what it was. The police enquiry had got precisely nowhere, in spite of all Chief Superintendent Blacker's experience and the distinguished assistance of the country's leading ballistics expert, Robert Churchill.

The Inquest was resumed on Friday, April 20th, but was again adjourned, while the police made one last ditch effort to solve the mystery. Blacker and Elliott joined their teams of detectives during the week as yet again they searched hedgerows and land adjoining the road from Bashall Eaves to Clitheroe. It is difficult to imagine that any clues now remained, but we can appreciate the police frustration. "Just one more look", they must have thought. Rumours had begun to circulate that the police were preparing to drop the case, but Blacker emphatically denied it. In spite of the public denials, he now realised that the trail was cold and the chances of finding anything new increasingly slim. The perpetrator of the crime had by now had plenty of time to cover his tracks and dispose of any suspicious evidence.

Reports concerning this baffling murder more or less cease in the local newspaper after April 27th 1934. By June 1st, Blacker had indeed given up. He wrote to Robert Churchill in London, *"I am afraid I have to confess, at last, that there seems no prospect of clearing up the Bashall Eaves crime."* He went on to say that they had done their best, *"but fell short of that little bit which would connect our man"*. Blacker added with typical Yorkshire bluntness that he hoped that the fact that the crime remained unsolved would be reflected in Churchill's bill for his services.

Robert Churchill replied, *"In such a case, where the deceased undoubtedly knew who killed him, but didn't talk, such a weight of evidence would be necessary to secure a conviction that perhaps you are fortunate in not having to prosecute."* Churchill actually made no charge at all for his services as he had not been required to appear as an expert witness in court.

The Inquest into the shooting of James Dawson had been adjourned on three separate occasions at the request of the West Riding Constabulary to enable them to continue their enquiries. With no prospect of any answers, it finally went ahead on 25th June 1934. The drama of the past three months was reflected in The Clitheroe Advertiser's headlines accompanying its inquest report:

BASHALL EAVES TRAGEDY

Shooting Mystery still Unsolved

Was the bullet shot from a catapult?
Inquest Verdict: Death from Bullet Wound; No Evidence as to Firing

The proceedings were attended by both Chief Superintendent Blacker and Inspector Elliott. For the first time, the statement made by Jim Dawson himself was heard, and detailed information about the police experimentation with various weapons, including the catapult, was put before the jury.

As the Inquest proceedings drew to a close after all the evidence had been given, the Coroner addressed the jury. He explained to them that their verdict must be on the evidence they had heard and that they must take care not be influenced by rumour as to how Jim Dawson's wound was caused. He added that there was no evidence to show how the bullet wound had been caused, the only evidence being Jim's statement that he did not know who fired the shot. The members of the jury could not, on that evidence, say how the bullet wound was caused.

The jury duly retired for a short time before returning an open verdict. Jim Dawson met his death from a bullet, there being no evidence to show how it was fired.

So, in spite of three months' hard work by a top detective and the country's leading ballistics expert, that was that. The murderer had got away with it.

PART TWO

THE QUEST FOR THE TRUTH

CHAPTER 6

Seeking the Ghost of Jim Dawson and the Missing Case File

JIM Dawson's murderer may have escaped justice in 1934, but the family could never entirely relinquish the hope that one day his killer's identity would be revealed. Wherever and whenever any snippets of potentially important information regarding his murder have found their way to our ears, we have followed them up, evaluated them and recorded them carefully.

We have for the most part, however, kept our own council as we evaluated the theories put forward by various television programmes in their attempts to identify the weapon, the motive and the possible perpetrator of the crime. Our reluctance to take part in these programmes was mainly due to my father Jack Lee's deep distrust of the media. As the 70th anniversary of Jim's murder began to loom, it seemed fitting that we should at last break our silence to correct the numerous errors and misconceptions which have crept into the story of Jim Dawson's life and death.

* * * * * * * * *

Over the past thirty years or so, the family has observed with some astonishment our relative's gradual transformation from murder victim into a focus of local myth and legend. This is, in no small part, due to his burgeoning career as a ghost.

The Ghost of Jim Dawson

Several books on the paranormal maintain that Jim's ghost goes a-haunting in Bashall Eaves. All of them get off to a very poor start by identifying the ghost concerned as John, rather than Jim Dawson. This includes Jack Hallam's 'The Ghost's Who's Who' (1977), within whose pages Jim would be surprised to find himself keeping company with such elevated personages as Anne Boleyn, Guy Fawkes and Oliver Cromwell. While the ghost of Queen Anne Boleyn walks the Tower of London, we are told that' John Dawson died leaving behind one of the biggest murder mysteries ever, and a ghost which searches for something in a hedge, near the gate where he was shot.

Presumably copying Jack Hallam's error, the ghost is again identified as John Dawson in Terence W. Whitaker's "Lancashire's Ghosts and Legends" (1980). Whitaker tells the story of Jim's murder with only a couple of very minor inaccuracies, and goes on to say that, *"Today there are many stories told of a squat figure, with a gaping wound showing through his tattered coat as he passes through the hedge near the farm, sometimes bending over, seeking in vain for the weapon and the person who used it. Is it any wonder that local people are not too keen on passing along the road taken by John Dawson on that fateful night in the spring of 1934?"*

Since 1980, Jim's ghost story has been all downhill. In a recent version he is described as John Dawson, a married farmer, who had been drinking at the Red Pump Hotel on the night he was shot. Upon discovering the wound in his back, his wife sent for an ambulance and Jim was taken to Blackburn Royal Infirmary where he died three days later. The ghost is again described as a 'squat figure', but now it is skulking pointlessly around the Red Pump*, with the added thrilling detail of bloodstains being clearly visible on its jacket. Jim and his ghost today appear to be in historical freefall.

In 2005 Jim has become a very up-to-date ghost, receiving an entry (again under the erroneous name of John Dawson) on a fascinating internet website known as the Paranormal Database where he is classified as a 'haunting manifestation'.

How ghost stories seem to develop a life of their own over the years is a fascinating subject. The Grey Lady of The Beacon House in Monken Hadley, Hertfordshire, whose story I investigated in the 1990s is a case in point and provides a good illustration of this phenomenon. The earliest version of the tale (from the 1940s) mentions merely a grey shadow floating up the stairs. The next report describes the apparition as a grey nun. A few years later, the ghost has become a grey nun walking upstairs carrying a mysterious cup. By 1997, however, a full-blown horror story had come into being. This described how a hunched nun of horrifying mien had been seen walking up the stairs carrying a bucket of blood!

The ghost of Jim Dawson seems to be heading in the same direction, new details being added to the story upon each re-telling. In a recent BBC Inside Out programme, broadcast on Monday 11th October, a local tour guide alleged that postal workers had witnessed Jim's ghost as a grey shape at the Brieryforth gate which was heard to utter the words, *"Why, why, why?"*

I first became aware of the tales of Jim Dawson's ghost in the late 1990s, when my sister Patricia came across the story by chance in Terence Whitaker's book. At this time I was, appropriately enough, about to publish a local history book in London, chronicling the career of the medieval Earl of Essex, Geoffrey de Mandeville who is North London's most famous phantom. I was fascinated to learn, after interviewing so many people about the ghost of Geoffrey, that a member of my own family was regarded as a ghost back in Lancashire. I therefore contacted the Clitheroe Advertiser and Times in the hope that local people could tell me more about Jim's ghost.

---

*The Red Pump is reputed to be haunted - but not by Jim Dawson.

The paper subsequently ran a story, "Jennie won't let this sleeping ghost lie!" on October 30th 1997 accompanied by a photograph of myself sitting on an iron ducking stool looking apprehensive*. According to the newspaper story, *"chilling reports abound of Jim Dawson's tormented ghost"* and it appealed for people to come forward and describe some sightings to me. Nobody ever did so.

Moving back to Lancashire in 2001 provided the opportunity to investigate Great-uncle Jim's ghost for myself and what better time to do so than on the 70th anniversary of his murder? This would serve the purpose of killing two birds with one stone. I could check out the murder scene at the appropriate time of year, while at the same time watch out for any spectral activity in the vicinity of the Brieryforth gate and Back Lane.

The Murder Scene, March 18th 2004

On the evening of March 18th 2004, therefore, I armed myself with a large, heavy torch (with which to hit any would-be assailants over the head) and left the house for the ten minute drive to Bashall Eaves. The weather that night was similar to the night of the shooting in 1934. It was extremely windy and dark, due to the heavy cloud cover, although the rain itself was very sporadic. Having duly arrived at the Brieryforth gate, and taken a right turn into Back Lane opposite the gate, I stopped the car thirty yards up the lane.

Here I switched off the headlights and got out of the car. I then waited five minutes or so for my eyes to accustom themselves to the gloom. By this time it was 9.15 p.m., the very time that Jim Dawson had heard the click and felt the sharp pain in his shoulder. I invited Jim to come and join me by softly saying his name a couple of times. He failed to answer my summons, so I increased the volume and roared his name several times very loudly. Still nothing. The ghost of my great-uncle stayed resolutely absent.

I cannot say that I was entirely surprised. The most common question I am asked when investigating local ghost stories is inevitably, *"Do you believe in ghosts?"* All I can say is that I have never personally encountered one. This is not for the want of trying. Over the past thirty years or so I have hung about in deserted passages under haunted castles in Normandy, loitered in Nero's eerie subterranean palace in Rome, lost the will to live in Geoffrey de Mandeville's fortress in South Mimms, crouched in dark crypts beneath medieval churches, and haunted graveyards too numerous to mention - all to no avail. Nobody dead ever wants to talk to me. And on 18th March 2004, I had to resign myself to the fact that this included members of my own family.

In the absence of Jim's ghost, I surveyed the murder scene. I suddenly noticed a shape padding silently towards me out of the murk from the direction of Bashall Town. Ah, Jim's ghost at last. But no, it was a large ginger and white cat. Strangely enough, during

---

*This ducking stool formed part of the private collection of Cecil Williamson, owner of the Museum of Witchcraft at Boscastle in Cornwall (recently badly damaged by flooding). Both my husband and Cecil seemed unreasonably keen that I try it out. It was very uncomfortable indeed.

a London 'Spookathon' organised by Marie Curie Cancer Care back in 1997, during which we held a midnight vigil in a graveyard to seek the ghost of Geoffrey de Mandeville, the only creature of the night which took any interest in us whatsoever was a very similar cat.

After the cat and I had made friends, we surveyed the scene together. It was extremely dark in Back Lane, the only illumination being afforded by the very dim glow of the distant lights of Clitheroe (which were presumably even less intense in 1934).

From where I was standing, the Brieryforth gate was completely invisible. As I walked towards the gate, it became visible from a distance of about four yards. I therefore concluded that it would have been next to impossible for anyone to have successfully aimed at and shot Jim from the Brieryforth gate if Jim had walked 30 yards up Back Lane, as he could not have been seen from that position. It would literally have been a shot in the dark. Indeed, when questioned at the Inquest about the visibility on the night of the shooting, both the local bobby, P.C. Sheldon, and Superintendent Elliott himself agreed that Jim could not have been seen from the Brieryforth gate if he had walked 30 yards up Back Lane.

If it was impossible to see Jim from 30 yards away, it seemed rather a pointless exercise, on the part of the police, to test the effectiveness of various weapons from a range of 30 yards. It strikes me as particularly futile when there was no evidence to suggest that the assailant had shot Jim from this position in the first place. He did state, of course, that he thought the man he had fleetingly seen standing at the Brieryforth gate (from 150 yards away) had been responsible for the attack. I cannot understand, however, why it should have been assumed that the man, if he was responsible, should still have been in that position when Jim Dawson arrived at the gate. Jim certainly never indicated that the lurking figure was still standing by the gate when he arrived there himself.

This visit to the murder scene on the 70th anniversary of the shooting was valuable in that it suggested very strongly to me that the assailant must have followed Jim up Back Lane and shot him from relatively close quarters in order to be able to see him in such dark conditions.

By now it was 9.40 p.m. and time to leave. After one last look around in case Jim's ghost had sneaked up behind me, I bade farewell to the cat, placed a waxy orchid in the hedge in Jim's memory, got in the car and drove home. While I have yet to meet anyone who claims to have seen Uncle Jim loitering in spirit form around Bashall Eaves, the ghost story has without doubt helped to maintain the high profile of this puzzling murder mystery and indeed has provided the final impetus needed for writing this book.

★ ★ ★ ★ ★ ★ ★ ★ ★

Ghosts aside, general media interest in the unsolved murder of Jim Dawson has remained consistently high. This is unsurprising as the case is both a criminologist's and amateur detective's dream, and as a result it has been the subject of two major television documentaries. The BBC's "Call the Gun Expert: The Perfect Crime" was broadcast in 1964, and was followed by Yorkshire TV's "The Village That Wouldn't Talk" in 1979.

The theories about the murder suggested in these programmes have had an enduring and significant effect on the way the murder is perceived in the Clitheroe and Bashall Eaves area. Local people have their own theories about the case, often said to be based on secret knowledge. Indeed, it is a popular saying in the Clitheroe area that, "Everybody knew who did it but nobody said." How far such assertions have been affected and contaminated by information received through the medium of television will shortly be examined, along with the theories suggested by the programmes themselves.

When I began to conduct my own research into the case, it became apparent that in order to assess fairly the merits of the various theories which had emerged over the years, new sources of information would be required. There were also a few question marks hanging over the sequence of events immediately after the shooting which needed to be addressed. I always realised that these questions could only be addressed realistically by gaining access to the original police evidence, but had little real expectation of ever being allowed access to Jim's case file. This was held, as far as the family knew, at Wakefield in West Yorkshire.

Little did I know, as I picked up the 'phone to call the West Yorkshire Police at Wakefield early in 2003 that it would be over a year before I finally tracked down the whereabouts of the written records relating to the murder of Jim Dawson.

Tracking down the Evidence

The family had always assumed that because the case was investigated by the West Riding Constabulary in 1934, the police file and exhibits (including the home-made bullet) had been safely stored at Wakefield since that time. Nobody had ever had the occasion to check that this was indeed the case. However, making this assumption turned out to be an extremely time-consuming error on my part.

It wasn't until most of the research into Jim's murder had already been gathered that any serious effort was made to locate the original evidence. Although I did not entertain any real hope of being allowed to consult the documents I had always, of course, been eager to do so. But at this stage it was far more a question of confirming the location of the file for the purposes of accuracy, and ascertaining if, after 70 years, the case was still considered to be 'live'.

Eventually, therefore, I got round to 'phoning the West Yorkshire Police Archive Service at Wakefield in 2003, to ask if they could verify that they held the case file, ballistics evidence and other exhibits relating to the murder of James Dawson in 1934. I fully expected a short delay while checks were made, and waited patiently for the call confirming the presence of the file and bullet.

Eventually, much to my alarm I received a call informing me that the staff could find no trace of any records of any description relating to the murder of James Dawson. They suggested that I contact my local County Record Office. The archivists at Preston were a little surprised to be asked if they held the records for an open murder case and assured me that they most certainly did not. In fact they had no information about the case whatsoever.

During a later conversation with West Yorkshire Police it transpired that the situation had been complicated by the amalgamation of several police forces over the years, and also by the fact that while Bashall Eaves had been in Yorkshire in 1934, it had been shifted into Lancashire during boundary changes in the 1970s. They could only suggest that I speak to the police at Lancashire Constabulary, to see if the murder file had been transferred into their custody.

Police officers of Lancashire Constabulary based at Preston and Blackburn were unable to assist me. They recommended that I speak to someone at Clitheroe C.I.D., Clitheroe Police Station having been the nearest one to the original crime scene. D.C. Proctor of Clitheroe C.I.D., while obviously suspecting I was mad, did everything in his power to assist when I turned up without warning on the station's doorstep. He was of the opinion that the North Yorkshire police were my best bet. Taking his advice, I consulted North Yorkshire Records Management Unit and C.I.D. headquarters, only to be told that Bashall Eaves had never fallen within their area.

I had therefore gone round in a circle and was back at square one. Locating the evidence, which I had expected to be so straightforward, was proving to be a frustrating nightmare.

However, I found it difficult to credit that the records of an open murder could have disappeared without trace, and resolved to carry on the quest by going back to the beginning and consulting the highest authorities possible. In August 2003 I therefore wrote to the Chief Constable of West Yorkshire Police outlining my query. I was contacted swiftly by the Chief Constable's secretary, who reiterated that Bashall Eaves had never fallen within their area. She also advised me that the police file on the case would have been deposited near the scene of the murder, and not at Wakefield. I was also told that I would not, in any case, be allowed to look at the files even if I managed to track them down.

While being fully aware that Clitheroe had never fallen within the West Riding of Yorkshire, the situation seemed so confused that I considered it worth making further enquiries with Lancashire Constabulary. To save time and avoid being repeatedly passed from pillar to post, I again went to the top and contacted Paul Stephenson, the Chief Constable of that force, on 13th October. Detective Chief Superintendent Paul Buschini subsequently got in touch with me on 21st October 2003. He had very kindly made a full search of the historical murder files currently held by the force. No trace of Jim's file had come to light. He, too, made the point that the file would never have moved far from the original murder enquiry headquarters.

It then occurred to me that while Chief Superintendent Blacker of Wakefield may have been in overall charge of the case, the actual headquarters for the investigation may well have been at Settle where Superintendent Elliott was based. This possibility was supported by the fact that my father and his cousin Albert were driven to Settle for interrogation back in 1934.

During a subsequent chat on the telephone, Paul Buschini suggested it might be worth calling the police station at Settle to see if the case file was still present there. Settle, he informed me, now fell within the area administered by the North Yorkshire Police Force. I tried to put out of my mind that I seemed to be chasing round in ever-decreasing circles. To cut a long story short, a search of the cellars of Settle police station revealed nothing more interesting than the heating boiler and a big angry spider. One of the members of staff informed me that they had recently had a big clear out and a lot of stuff had been taken to Skipton. A call to Skipton police station had negative results, and a somewhat a bemused member of staff eventually recommended that I email their Chief Constable, Della Cannings, to see if she could solve the mystery of the whereabouts of the file.

By this time I was tired and fed up (though possibly not as tired and fed up as the ever-polite and long-suffering police officers on the receiving end of my persistent pestering). As a last ditch attempt to locate the murder file, I emailed Della Cannings on 12th November 2003.

An email arrived from a member of her team, Inspector Richard Spedding, on 19th November containing wonderful news. *"I am pleased to tell you that I have traced the file. I have not looked at it yet, so cannot say if we have the bullet or not."*

I was extremely impressed, not to mention astounded that after so many years and after so many police force amalgamations the North Yorkshire Police had managed to locate the documentation. Believing in striking while the iron was hot, I tentatively asked if I might be allowed to look at the documents. I was informed that this was entirely possible.

It was not all good news, unfortunately. I was troubled and disappointed to learn shortly afterwards that the bullet which was responsible for Jim's death did not appear to be present with the case notes. Also missing were the photographs, police maps, X-ray and the clothes Jim had been wearing on the night he was shot. All these items seemed to have disappeared without trace, which meant that my quest to locate the original evidence had to continue.

I had been particularly eager to track down the whereabouts of the bullet in case a potential murder weapon ever came to light. If we remember, the bullet was made of hard steel with distinctive markings which would in all likelihood have marked the barrel of the gun which fired it. Without the bullet, the firm identification of a potential murder weapon would be impossible.

In the meantime, however, Christina Scaife, of North Yorkshire Police Information Compliance Unit emailed the magnificent news that I would be allowed a day, under constant supervision, to consult the original witness statements at their headquarters at Newby Wiske, near Northallerton. The appointment was eventually scheduled for ten o'clock on the morning of Wednesday, 11th February 2004.

The Visit to Newby Wiske

Realising I would have only limited time with the files on 11th February, and that the drive would waste at least four hours of the day, I decided to maximise my time by driving to Newby Wiske the day before and staying overnight in the village.

I awoke on the morning of Tuesday, 10th February with mixed feelings of apprehension and anticipation. The trepidation was caused by the thought of the journey facing me that day. To explain - I hate travelling on my own and absolutely detest driving at the best of times, even when I know where I am going (which isn't very often). Signposts flash past before I get the chance to read them. I effortlessly become hopelessly lost at the drop of a hat. My mother and I once found ourselves dazed and confused in an Italian town which had only one street. Indeed it was commented in Barnet, North London (where I lived and worked in the local museum for 20 years) that I was quite capable of losing my bearings not only in Barnet itself but even within the confines of my own museum. Maps are a no-no. I cannot make head nor tail of them. I was, then, dreading the journey to North Yorkshire. With my track record, I might very well end up in Scotland.

As it turned out, a guardian angel must have installed a navigational aid in my brain that day. I somehow found my way across the dark, foggy and largely deserted moors without any trouble, pausing occasionally to scan the horizon expectantly for passing werewolves. I only became lost within 15 yards or so of the North Yorkshire police headquarters in the village of Newby Wiske itself. Unable to spot any sign of my hotel in the small village, I asked a passing policewoman who had conveniently stopped because I had almost run her over, the way to the Solberge Hall Hotel. She pointed to a track leading out of the village into the middle of nowhere, which was not encouraging.

I need not have worried as the hotel was an elegant and peaceful country retreat, built on the site of both a Viking sacrificial site and Benedictine monastery. A slight problem was encountered, however, when the friendly staff showed me to a no-smoking room. I wasn't having any of that. I was immediately transferred to a wonderful suite of rooms which gave every appearance of being more extensive than my own house, complete with chaise longue, canopied bed and stunning views. I passed the evening making frequent calls to room service while lolling upon the magnificent bed reading "The Return of the King" by J.R.R. Tolkien, and trying to fool myself into believing that I was enjoying it. I then settled down to sleep hoping that a handsome blond elf (or failing that, the ghost of a Viking) might drop by and wake me up for a chat. No such luck.

The next morning, after an excellent breakfast, I checked out of the Solberge Hall Hotel (which I cannot recommend too highly) and made the five minute journey to the unexpectedly splendid building and grounds which house North Yorkshire Police Headquarters in the village. Christina Scaife met me at the door, and ushered me through to a conference room just off the canteen.

It was only really at this juncture that it hit me that I was about to see documents I had dreamed of consulting for many years, most of which had probably not seen the light of day or been handled or examined by anyone since 1934. As the enormous box marked 'The Murder of James Dawson, 1934' was placed in front of me, I felt closer to Jim than I had ever thought possible. It was a very emotional moment when I picked up the first witness statement and discovered it to be that given by my father so many years ago.

I had set out from home with some specific questions to which I hoped the files would provide some answers. For example, I thought it would be useful to establish who had been drinking in the Edisford Bridge Hotel on the night of March 18th 1934. I was particularly keen also to read the original statements given by Tommy Simpson of Bashall Town, Tommy Kenyon, the farmhand at Bashall Hall, and the statements given by members of Jim Dawson's close family. Other documents I was anxious to consult were the post-mortem report and the X-ray report concerning the dog which had been shot and subsequently exhumed by the police. I hoped to be able to find and read these particular documents carefully, and also have time to skim-read through every piece of paper present in order to provide myself with an overall picture of the murder investigation.

Alas, this aim proved to be far too ambitious and ultimately impossible. Hundreds of documents faced me, every one of which was of great interest and it proved to be an unfeasible task to scan, let alone read carefully through every one of them. While the police would, without doubt, have been happy to arrange another day's visit, my financial situation at this time meant that this was not an option. Another day with the file would not have made that much difference in any case. I craved months of access to the information. I had to content myself, however, with getting through as much as possible in the time very kindly allowed to me by the North Yorkshire Police on 11th February and am eternally grateful to the force for allowing me any access to the case file at all. As luck would have it, I was fortunate enough to find the answers to all the specific questions I had prepared and discovered other very useful and interesting information besides, much of which has been utilised in the reconstruction of the events of March - June 1934.

Having thanked Christina Scaife for all her help, I enquired for how much longer the case would be considered 'live' and thus open to investigation should new evidence ever come to light. The answer to this question came, *'For ever.'*

The Missing Evidence

After a marathon bombardment of 'phone calls, letters and emails, the case file relating to the murder of Jim Dawson had at last been located safe and sound in North Yorkshire. The same could not be said, however, of the home-made bullet which had been responsible for his death, or indeed the rest of the exhibits.

As soon as it became apparent that the distinctive bullet (along with who knows what else) had at some point become separated from the witness statements, I had initiated enquiries into its whereabouts. It seemed surprising, to say the least, that such an important piece of evidence as a bullet should have gone missing from the file of an undetected murder case. If it had indeed vanished then I could personally see little point in the enquiry remaining open.

My initial thought was that its disappearance might well have something to do with the fact that in 1934 the ballistics evidence had been sent down to London to the gun expert, Robert Churchill. Had the bullet and the rest of the evidence ever, in fact, returned to the North? If the bullet had stayed in London, what had happened to it? Research revealed that the journalist Macdonald Hastings had inherited many of Robert Churchill's effects after the gun expert's death in 1958.

Born on 6th October 1909, Macdonald Hastings was the editor of The Strand magazine. This was a showcase for new fiction between 1946 and 1950, and featured stories by H.G.Wells, Conan Doyle and P.G.Woodhouse amongst others. He was also the founding editor of Country Fair magazine and acted as war correspondent for the London "Picture Post". A prolific writer, Mr. Hastings had five detective novels and 20 non-fiction books to his credit. He also edited two books about game shooting, and was a frequent radio and television broadcaster.

Published in 1963, "The Other Mr. Churchill" was Macdonald Hastings' biography of Robert Churchill; this devoted a substantial section to the murder of Jim Dawson. While I could recite the information it contained about the murder itself almost by rote, I had never had any reason to hunt through it for information concerning Robert Churchill's death, and the fate of his personal effects.

Upon reading the book from cover to cover, I discovered some information which alarmed me. Macdonald Hastings commented that in Robert Churchill's will he was left his papers and a *black museum* of exhibits. He went on to say that he was faced with hundreds of items stuffed any old how into ammunition boxes or crammed into sacks. These included old case files Churchill had worked on and an armament of test bullets, mostly unidentified and covered with corrosion.

The suspicion that Macdonald Hastings may have inherited the bullet which killed Jim Dawson was further aroused upon viewing a videotape of his 1964 BBC drama-documentary, "Call the Gun Expert: The Perfect Crime" in the spring of 2004. During the course of the programme Mr. Hastings held up a large bullet to the camera. This he identified to the viewer as the actual bullet which had killed Jim Dawson. Also featured were police maps of the crime scene, along with Robert Churchill's notebooks relating to the case and also his correspondence with Chief Superintendent Blacker.

This seemed to be fairly compelling evidence that Macdonald Hastings had indeed been in possession of the bullet in 1964. However, I was not entirely convinced. I could see no reason for the West Riding Constabulary to have sent other items down to London which had also disappeared, such as Jim's clothing. A careful check through the Inquest evidence provided the final confirmation that I had been on a wild goose chase.

For at the Inquest on 25th June 1934 it was stated that, *"The bullet that wounded Dr. Bailey* [the police surgeon] *along with that which wounded Mr. Dawson,* was handed for inspection to the Jury."

The bullet which Macdonald Hastings held up (twice!) for the viewers' inspection, claiming that it was the actual missile which had killed Jim Dawson can therefore have been no such thing because the genuine article had been present in Blackburn at the Inquest in June 1934. By this time, Robert Churchill's part in the investigation had already ended and he had obviously returned the evidence to the West Riding Constabulary in time for the Inquest. Macdonald Hastings could not, therefore, have inherited the bullet from Churchill. "Call the Gun Expert: The Perfect Crime" was made in the style of a drama-documentary. Unfortunately this resulted in the programme making no distinction at all between what was fact and what was fiction, both of which were freely and misleadingly intermingled within the programme.

However, although I no longer believed Macdonald Hastings had ever been in possession of the bullet which killed Jim Dawson, it seemed that he had certainly inherited some interesting paperwork which might contain further information about the case. What had happened to these items when Macdonald Hastings himself died in 1982? A quick bit of research on the internet revealed that the famous Sir Max Hastings, former editor of the London Evening Standard, was the son of Macdonald Hastings. In May 2004 I received an email from Sir Max informing me that all his father's effects had been donated to an American university. As this had happened over twenty years ago he could not, alas, remember to which university it had been bequeathed.

I seemed to have reached a dead end, as there are rather a lot of American universities and it would be a mammoth task to contact all of them individually. However, I never give up without a fight. On the internet search engine I tried typing in the keywords 'Macdonald Hastings American Universities'. Little which seemed relevant came up, apart from a mention of Macdonald Hastings' name at the University of Texas. I therefore emailed the University of Texas enquiring whether or not they held any of Macdonald Hastings' personal effects. I received an email from Tara at the university on 4th June which stated: *I'm afraid the collection did not come to the Ransom Centre. The only lead I could find for you is a Macdonald Hastings Collection at Boston University, Mugat Memorial Library, Special Collections Department, 771 Commonwealth Avenue, Boston MA 02215.*

On 22nd June I received an email from the University of Boston. *"The reference request you have sent regarding the Macdonald Hastings Collection is a detailed and complex one. The inventory listing on file is of a broad nature. While it lists nothing specific, it does indicate that there is some Robert Churchill material. As this material is stored off-site we were not able to pull the actual boxes to see the nature of the files.*

To fully answer your question, it would be best for you to schedule a visit to the archives or hire a proxy researcher to do the research for you."

It seems therefore that some very interesting papers and correspondence relating to the murder of Jim Dawson may well have ended up at the bottom of a crate in Boston, U.S.A. How very frustrating!

While this was all very interesting, it had got me no further in my quest to locate the home-made bullet. Bearing in mind that after the Inquest had taken place in June 1934 the bullet and other exhibits might have ended up anywhere, I decided to widen the scope of my enquiries.

My first port of call was the Crime Museum (formerly the Black Museum) at Scotland Yard. This was a long shot, but seemed worth a 'phone call. I was aware that the museum held some unexpected items, having once tracked down to this location some illegal gaming boards confiscated at Barnet Fair in the nineteenth century. After a few frustrating months of unacknowledged messages, however, I eventually learned that the Crime Museum held no evidence relating to the murder of James Dawson in 1934.

Detective Chief Inspector Buschini of Lancashire Constabulary then suggested that I contact the North West Forensic Science Service as a potential depository for the bullet. This proved to be a dead end. I also contacted, on the advice of North Yorkshire Police, the police museum at Ripon. The curator, Ralph Lindley, was horrified at the very idea that anyone might think the museum held important murder evidence, and quickly assured me that it did not. We did have a very interesting chat about the case, however.

That proved to be the end of the road in my quest to locate the bullet and other exhibits relating to the murder of Jim Dawson. I could think of nowhere else to look for them. Their whereabouts is now extremely uncertain and they can probably be presumed lost during all the police force amalgamations and boundary changes which have taken place. This is most regrettable, but these things happen. Unfortunately, however, if there was ever any real chance of solving the 'cold case' of the murder of Jim Dawson utilising 21st century police methods, this must unquestionably have depended upon the preservation, in perfect condition, of both the case file and the exhibits.

Perhaps the only real hope of new light ever being thrown upon this intriguing historical murder now rests on the possibility that a resident of Bashall Eaves might eventually volunteer *bona fide* information which has hitherto been concealed. Regrettably, however, genuine local memory of the Jim Dawson case has been seriously contaminated by media involvement over the past forty years, as we are now about to discover.

CHAPTER 7

Bashall Eaves and the Wall of Silence: *Theories Old and New*

AS soon as Jim Dawson died of septicaemia in a Blackburn Nursing Home on 22nd March 1934, some very inventive ideas began to emerge concerning the murder weapon, the motive and the possible identity of his killer.

Armed with valuable information gleaned from the original witness statements to supplement the many years of personal research, I now felt reasonably qualified to analyse the diverse theories which have surfaced over the years concerning the murder of my great-uncle. The time has now come to consider these theories upon their individual merits.

An Accident?

The accidental shooting scenario was aired by the Blackburn Coroner, Mr. T. R. Thompson in his summing up at the Inquest in June, 1934. He commented to the jury, *"You may well come to the conclusion that somebody made that bullet and, wishing to try it, fired it in a barn, perhaps 500 or 600 yards away, and that the bullet travelled that distance and struck deceased."*

A similar idea was mooted in 1980 by my ex-husband Nick Cobban, a former investigative journalist who studied the case in some detail. More recently, crime expert Vincent Burke, to whom I spoke about the case on BBC Inside Out in July 2004, came up with the same idea. Their 'accident' theory is very similar to that of the Coroner and proposes that Jim was not murdered at all but shot unintentionally by a stray bullet fired by someone who just happened to be out shooting that night. If this was the case, then the bullet could have been fired from some distance away, from the direction of Brieryforth or Thirty Acres Farm, and hit Jim Dawson quite by chance.

This theory would mean that a more conventional firearm could have fired the home-made bullet. It would also explain why no motive for the murder could be established. There wasn't one. But the question still remains; why fashion a home-made bullet and fire it from an ordinary gun when conventional ammunition was readily available? And who would be out shooting at that time of night in such wild, wet and windy weather?

It is tempting to suggest that poachers were on the loose, but as far as I am aware, it was rather early in the year for poaching activities. I personally find this theory a little far-fetched, but it can certainly not be ruled out as a possibility.

I have recently been told about another theory, however, which is so far-fetched that it verges on the desperate. It postulates that Jim himself was out poaching that night and shot himself by mistake. Er, in the back? My great-uncle Jim Dawson was neither a criminal nor a contortionist, and this is a very silly theory indeed.

A Joke involving a Catapult?

Could Jim have died as the result of a stupid prank that went wrong? We have already established that some of the young men in Bashall Eaves thought it a bit of a lark to play senseless and disrespectful practical jokes, even when a murder investigation was in full swing. The idea that the assault on Jim Dawson may have been a malicious attack carried out by a local youth armed with a catapult was certainly one which the Coroner felt worth exploring at the Inquest. The police also took the idea seriously.

Perhaps Jim Dawson was not particularly well-liked by the local teenagers, and for all we know a trivial incident may have taken place involving Jim scolding one of them for some minor misdemeanour. The youth (or youths) concerned may have taken a very adolescent revenge, lying in wait for Jim on his way home from the pub and then firing the bullet at him from a catapult - not to kill, but merely to give him a painful shock. It is unlikely that any of the young men, when interviewed by the police, would admit to having a problem with Jim in view of his unexpected death.

So what, realistically, are the pros and cons of a catapult as the mystery murder weapon? First of all, a catapult certainly makes the right noise when it is fired - a click. Secondly, Jim himself brought up the idea of a catapult the morning after he had been shot. And thirdly we have the evidence placed before the jury at the Inquest by Superintendent Elliott, who had tested the efficacy of a catapult during his experiments. It is worth reminding ourselves of the Inquest evidence here.

> "*The Coroner: Assuming the bullet was fired from a catapult, what would be the effect?*
>
> *Superintendent Elliott: It would have had a similar result as that on the deceased. A bullet, similar to the one taken from the deceased's shoulder, discharged from a catapult at 30 yards range, passed through three thicknesses of cloth, two pieces of linen, and made a dent in a tin plate. The cloth is similar to that worn by Mr. Dawson that night.*
>
> *Superintendent Elliott exhibited the tin plate, covered with the cloth and linen, and pointed out the dent caused in the plate. He also produced a catapult and showed that on being discharged it made a noise which could be described as a click."*

While the above exercise may seem reasonable at first glance, the point does have to be made that as a scientific experiment, it leaves a lot to be desired. A tin plate is hardly comparable to a human body. Also, we are not told the size of the tin plate, nor how many attempts were made to hit this target from 30 yards away. It cannot have been an easy challenge. During a break in recent filming for B.B.C. Inside Out, the cameraman, Ken Ward, suggested to me that it would be next to impossible to fire any bullet-shaped missile with any accuracy using a catapult. The bullet would drift, and 'tumble' towards its target. The chances of its business end penetrating the victim's body would therefore be miniscule.

But the main objection to the catapult theory has to be the bullet itself. If the intention was merely to give Jim a painful shock as he walked home, why fire a large home-made bullet at him rather than a stone?

The first to come up with original hypotheses concerning both the motive and the murder weapon was the journalist Macdonald Hastings. His thoughts about the murder of Jim Dawson first saw the light of day in his 1963 biography of the gun expert, Robert Churchill, called "The Other Mr. Churchill". A year later the book was adapted by the B.B.C. into a television programme entitled, "Call the Gun Expert: The Perfect Crime".

This was an influential programme; for in addition to proposing new ideas about the case, it was largely responsible for disseminating, if not actually creating, the idea that Bashall Eaves was an extremely secretive and backward community. The effects of this programme remain only too apparent to any researcher attempting to study the Jim Dawson case today.

"Call the Gun Expert: The Perfect Crime" (B.B.C. 1964) (The jealous husband or angry father theory)

Thirty years after the murder of Jim Dawson and broadcast on 6th August, 1964, "The Perfect Crime" was the last of six programmes in a series entitled "Call the Gun Expert" featuring famous murder cases in which the gun expert Robert Churchill had been involved. The series was narrated by journalist and broadcaster Macdonald Hastings and based upon the private papers bequeathed to him by Robert Churchill when he died in 1958 at the age of 72. It was an innovative piece of television which is now regarded as virtually the first example of a drama-documentary series.

Even today, the high quality of the programme shines through, although its style and approach seem very dated indeed to a 21st century audience. In the dramatised sections of the programme, Robert Churchill, the gun expert, was played by the actor Wensley Pithey, while the part of Jim Dawson was taken by Alan Hockey and the shadowy killer at the Brieryforth gate, looking for all the world like Nosferatu, was portrayed by Patrick Travis.

The contrast in the accents employed by the actors portraying 'authority' figures such as Churchill, and the 'natives' as represented by Jim Dawson himself, might well strike today's viewer as rather comical. (I certainly laughed.) Churchill is 'ever so posh' while Jim's Yorkshire (?) accent can be cut with a knife and is so thick as to be almost incomprehensible.

The programme was presented by Macdonald Hastings in person, who said in the Radio Times (25th June 1964), *"My own part in the series, as narrator, involves me in two dimensions of time. I am playing myself, the contemporary reporter of the Tonight programme, as if I was present when the casebooks were unfolding all those years ago."*

As he sets the scene, Mr. Hastings contemplates Bashall Eaves and its inhabitants with an air of polite and well-bred perplexity, while dutifully building up the atmosphere for his murder mystery in much the same way as a crime novelist would approach the subject. As portrayed in "The Perfect Crime", the beautiful countryside of the Ribble Valley has an unnaturally bleak, inhospitable and sinister look about it. The local residents are described as the people in the shadow of Pendle Hill, home of the Lancashire witches, where centuries of inbreeding had seen to it that village idiots were in plentiful supply. In this closed rural community, *"Families were so numerous and in surname so few that individuals could only be identified by their nicknames."*

Macdonald Hastings states that at the time of Jim Dawson's murder, traces of the medieval guilds system were still to be found in the area. It is difficult to determine precisely what he is implying by this statement. Possibly he is referring to a survival of something resembling an old guild at Mitton parish church.

In late medieval England, these parish guilds resembled religious social clubs. Members, often in the same profession, paid a fee and ensured that proper funerals were available to all their associates and that a priest was available to say mass. They also banded together to provide charitable services (for example schooling) both for their members and for the wider parish community.

Certainly some members of the congregation of Mitton church, notably Tommy Simpson of Bashall Town Farm, appeared to be heavily involved at the time of the murder in an attempt to close down Bashall Eaves village school and transfer its pupils to the school at Mitton. This situation led to some very peculiar exchanges in a local newspaper.

The local schoolmistress Eleanor Booth complained bitterly on April 13th 1934 that *"The person who is unfortunate enough to accept the post of head teacher at Bashall Eaves school is made the target and butt of the spleen and vindictiveness of a clique determined to oppose education and all it stands for. Even my private life is interfered with and endeavours made to make the school house untenable. These attacks are from men who are adept at bullying women. The most cordial relationship has always existed between myself and the parents. But when children leave this school insidious and foul mischief is instilled into them. A recreation room here admits boys of any age,* [which] *is not under supervision and is made use of by disciples of the clique to encourage and stimulate unhealthy excitement."*

In a reference to the murder of Jim Dawson, she added, *"In view of the recent tragic happening and the conditions prevailing, it is up to the parents to proceed with the protest they launched and get some responsible persons to help to promote social life and conditions in keeping with the 20th century and not with feudal times."*

It is highly probable that Macdonald Hastings (or his local researcher) was aware of these enigmatic and rather disturbing remarks in the Clitheroe Advertiser and Times in April 1934 alleging that Bashall Eaves still had one foot in The Middle Ages. It is possible, therefore, that he based his even stranger allegations of the survival of medieval guilds upon the comments made by the village schoolmistress, Eleanor Booth, or that he had followed up some information (possibly regarding local Freemasonry) which has escaped my notice.

In "The Perfect Crime", Jim Dawson himself is portrayed as the stereotypical 'Farmer Dawson', a very stout individual living with one sister in a dark, basic and poky farmhouse, which had interior walls of rough-hewn stone. How the programme-makers reconciled the interior shots of this peculiar version of Farmer Dawson's house with their exterior shots, which showed the actor driving up to the imposing medieval residence of Bashall Hall itself, is one of the puzzles of the programme. Equally puzzling is Macdonald Hastings' assertion that it was a well-known saying in the area that no male member of the Dawson family had ever died at Bashall Hall. This was news to us, and for a moment my son Daniel was thrilled, believing that he was implying that the Dawson men were vampires rather than that they had all died elsewhere. Macdonald Hastings seemed to be totally unaware of the blood-soaked history of Bashall Hall itself, which is probably just as well.

Mr. Hastings stated quite erroneously in the programme that the case of Jim Dawson was closed. He further asserted that when the police investigation into Jim's murder began, their enquiries ran into a local stone wall of silence in this village, which he describes as one of the closest and most secretive communities in the land. In such communities, *"Country folk don't like telling tales to foreigners about people they have to live with, and anyone from 10 miles away was a foreigner in Bashall Eaves."*

In case any viewer was still missing the point, he added that the police had more chance of getting information out of the local sheep than the local inhabitants. The programme also strongly implied that the locals knew who had committed the crime, but kept it to themselves.

It would be as well to bear in mind here that in the reporting of any unsolved village murder, it appears to be almost convention to highlight the problem of secretive villagers who know more than they will say. Bashall Eaves is certainly not the only 'village that wouldn't talk' about its local murder. During the investigation into the so-called 'Witchcraft Murder' of Charles Walton of Lower Quinton, Warwickshire in 1945, for example, the famous Detective Superintendent Fabian of Scotland Yard was faced with *'a barrage of silence from anyone questioned about it'*.

In a recent investigation by BBC Coventry, the reporter found the people of Lower Quinton *'friendly but tight-lipped'*. One village resident told her, *"Talking about it would upset people and there's no sense in alienating people in a small village like this."* Another added, *"In cases like this there's always someone that knows something. Someone knows what happened but for the sake of relatives and for not upsetting people, no-one will say."* Finally the reporter was informed that there were still people for whom the event is more than legend but they will not talk.

The attitudes allegedly displayed by the inhabitants of Bashall Eaves in Lancashire are thus remarkably similar to those of the residents of Lower Quinton deep in the Warwickshire countryside.

What was (and still is) probably a common reaction to outsiders in the countryside has thus, perhaps, over-emphasised and transformed into something far more sinister and secretive than it really was for dramatic effect. To be fair, however, there seems to be very little doubt that there was at least a germ of truth in Macdonald Hastings' depiction of Bashall Eaves and its environs in 1934. As we have seen, the young men of the village went in for playing idiotic and inappropriate practical jokes, and it is certainly the case that the people in the area are historically notorious for resenting what they see as interference in their local affairs by outsiders. While this may be excused as a common countryside reaction to strangers, it became, nonetheless, totally unacceptable when it included police officers attempting to investigate a murder within the community. And today it unquestionably remains the case that certain individuals have, quite inexplicably, kept quiet about potential new evidence in this old murder case, as we will see.

Every programme of this type needs to have an original slant on its subject matter. Having set the scene of a Bashall Eaves bearing a marked resemblance to the disturbing and inbred communities featured in the films Straw Dogs and Deliverance, "The Perfect Crime" showed dramatised reconstructions of what might have happened on the night of 18th March[*] 1934.

We see the actor playing Jim Dawson leaving the Edisford Bridge Hotel and walking along the Clitheroe Road to the Brieryforth[†] gate. Here he notices briefly a sinister-looking man lurking in the shadows. Jim is then joined by an unidentified 'mistress'. The two have a brief conversation as they walk along during which it is strongly implied that this mystery woman is pregnant. The attacker then springs out of the shadows and shoots Jim at point blank range with a weapon known as a Poacher's Arm as the woman runs away. Jim is then seen staggering off down Back Lane, clutching frantically at his back. The reconstruction suggests, therefore, that Jim was murdered by either the angry father, or the jealous boyfriend or husband of the 'mistress'.

This was ostensibly an original idea for a possible murder motive, and caused great interest in the Bashall Eaves and Clitheroe area. No mention had been made by the local newspapers in 1934 that Jim had been a bit of a ladies' man and therefore the motive suggested in the programme seemed a novel one. Macdonald Hastings appeared to base his idea on a supposed comment made by Robert Churchill however, rather than any specific new research into the events of 1934. He says in his book "The Other Mr. Churchill" that the gun expert had recommended to the Chief Constable of the West Riding that his detectives should "Cherchez la femme". However as we saw earlier, the police began to investigate Jim Dawson's love life on the very night he died, and were therefore already looking for a female connection before Churchill had been called into the case.

---

[*] The programme mistakenly states that the crime took place on 19th March.
† Brieryforth is pronounced incorrectly throughout the programme.

Be that as it may, the motive of jealousy as suggested in "The Perfect Crime" is a feasible one and worthy of serious consideration. We have already described Jim's liaison with Lily Barker along with the police suspicions regarding Nancy Simpson. Moreover, Jim may have had several liaisons about which the family and police knew nothing in 1934.

Indeed within the past ten years the family have been informed that Jim Dawson had one girlfriend about whom we previously knew nothing. This woman was linked, we were told, with a public house called The King's Arms, in an area of Clitheroe known as Bawdlands*. According to our source, she had jilted Jim because she had become tired of waiting for him to marry her. A check through the original evidence at North Yorkshire Police Headquarters confirmed that no woman connected with this public house appeared upon the police list of the women associated with Jim Dawson.

As well as coming up with a feasible murder motive, Macdonald Hastings also brought to the attention of the wider public his idea that the murder weapon had been an old-fashioned weapon known as an air cane, or Poacher's Arm. Since the programme was aired, memories have become a little hazy and many people now seem to be under the impression that the theory originated with the gun expert himself, Robert Churchill.

This is quite mistaken for as Hastings pointed out, Robert Churchill knew everything there was to know about conventional firearms, but had no experience whatsoever of air canes. It is Macdonald Hastings himself who must take the credit for having noticed the words 'air cane' in a scribbled list of weapons in one of Robert Churchill's handwritten notebooks, and following it up. Churchill himself did not appear to pursue the idea in 1934, and seemed to make no strong recommendation to the police that they should be putting all their energies into seeking such a weapon.

People invariably believe what they see on television and since the programme was aired in 1964, it has become almost received wisdom that an air cane was indeed the mystery weapon employed in the murder of Jim Dawson.

A minor problem with Macdonald Hastings theory, however, is the noise made when a Poacher's Arm is fired. When Jim Dawson was shot, he said he heard a click - the same sort of sound that a catapult would make. An air cane, when it was fired by Macdonald Hastings in the programme, produced an unusual noise. It is a difficult sound to describe - perhaps more like a muffled crack than a click. Did Jim himself find it difficult to describe what he had heard on that wild and windy night and choose the word 'click' as the nearest approximation to the sound? While not fully convinced, I consider that Macdonald Hastings was certainly on the right lines with his air cane theory.

"The Perfect Crime" went down like a lead balloon with the residents of Bashall Eaves. On August 14th 1964, the Clitheroe Advertiser and Times voiced the community's exasperation with the way the area had been portrayed in the programme.

---

*A corruption of Baldwin's Lands and nothing to do with bawds or brothels!

The report stated, *"The programme did imply, much to the annoyance of the Bashall Eaves residents in particular, that Bashall Eaves was not only a close-knit community but a peculiarly backward one where the people treated anyone from 10 miles away as foreigners. The version of the affair...was filmed in February when the countryside looked very bleak and wild, giving the impression that Bashall Eaves...was in the remotest and bleakest part of Britain. The programme stated that the villagers were unco-operative with the police and that 'someone must know something' but no-one would come forward, giving the impression that Bashall Eaves people were a strange tribe who did not venture from the hills except in raiding parties."*

However the reputation of the village of Bashall Eaves as a backward and secretive community which maintained a wall of silence about the murder of Jim Dawson was now a matter of record, and Macdonald Hastings' programme was to provide a blueprint for media treatment of the case in the future. The residents of Bashall Eaves may not have appreciated Hastings' portrayal of their village, but they were now well and truly stuck with their weird reputation whether they liked it or not.

"The Perfect Crime" had extremely serious consequences for anyone attempting to research the murder of Jim Dawson. Once the programme had been aired, it became increasingly difficult to ascertain if information offered by local people about the murder was genuine memory, or merely a garbled memory of what they, or their parents, had seen on television or read in local newspapers. The contamination of historical evidence concerning the events of 1934 was now well underway. And things were about to get a whole lot worse.

"The Village that Wouldn't Talk" (1979)
(The Mistaken Identity Theory)

The second major TV investigation into the unsolved murder of Jim Dawson arrived on our television screens 15 years later. This was Yorkshire Television's 1979 production of "The Village That Wouldn't Talk". There are no prizes for guessing to which village the title was referring. While no doubt a very entertaining piece of television, the programme has unfortunately been responsible for introducing, albeit inadvertently, a vast amount of erroneous detail into the story surrounding the murder of Jim Dawson. Today, many of these factual errors are still regarded as the truth.

The documentary was narrated by a police newspaper editor called Barry Shaw who, we are told, had been fascinated by this classic murder mystery for ten years. According to Mr. Shaw in his introductory comments, the body of James Dawson was laid to rest in the local graveyard 'but not in peace'. He added that any visitors to his grave were more likely to be criminologists than relatives. Jim's family, who tend his grave, received this information in stony silence.

In the course of the programme, the story of Jim's murder and the subsequent investigation was recounted, and we are told that it was Robert Churchill himself who came up with the theory that the mystery murder weapon was an air cane, or Poacher's Arm.

This, as we have seen, is not strictly accurate. However, it provided yet another excuse to mount a demonstration of this fascinating weapon in action.

Bashall Eaves was once again portrayed as a village of tight-lipped farming folk, who knew a lot more than they told the police in 1934. During the programme Barry Shaw briefly interviewed Chief Superintendent Wilfred Blacker, the detective in charge of the Jim Dawson case. He described the Bashall Eaves residents as stubborn types who would never give anybody away. It would have been interesting to hear more from Mr. Blacker than the couple of sentences that made it into the programme.

We also saw Barry Shaw attempting to question busy Bashall Eaves residents about the murder, and receiving a uniformly hostile response. This reaction was presumably, of course, what the programme-makers were looking for. Enquiries have revealed that some local residents who were fully prepared to talk about the murder were disregarded, while others who were interviewed did not appear in the programme. I have even heard that one potential contributor, after expressing willingness to share her memories of the murder, was subsequently asked if she would mind stating to the camera that she didn't want to talk about it!

All this was presumably to provide a sense of awed surprise when, in spite of the unhelpful attitude of the locals, the programme-makers managed to run to earth a man who was prepared not only to talk about the murder, but also to provide them with a new slant on the mystery and a potential suspect to boot.

This man was none other than Tommy Kenyon of Cardigan Street, Preston, who had been Jim Dawson's farm labourer at Bashall Hall back in 1934. It was his contention that the shooting of Jim Dawson was a case of mistaken identity*. He strongly implied that Tommy Simpson of Bashall Town Farm was responsible for the murder, and had shot Jim Dawson by mistake thinking it was Kenyon himself. The motive, he alleged, was Simpson's suspicion that he, Tommy Kenyon, had been responsible for the unwanted pregnancy of his daughter, Nancy Simpson.

The story told by Tommy Kenyon to Yorkshire Television in 1979 was riddled with serious factual errors from beginning to end. His version of events has long been accepted as trustworthy and accurate, even in the area around Bashall Eaves itself. Along with Yorkshire Television in 1979, the general public, quite understandably, accepted him as a reliable witness who knew what he was talking about because he was living in the same house as Jim Dawson at the time the murder took place. And as I have said before, people believe what they are told on the television.

However, as we will see, the information given to Barry Shaw by Tommy Kenyon often flatly contradicts not only the police evidence, the Inquest and family statements, but his own statements made in 1934 as well. It is vital, therefore, that any future researchers into the Jim Dawson case realise that Tommy Kenyon was an unreliable source of information. It is now time to set the record straight.

---

* An idea already mentioned briefly at the Inquest and by Macdonald Hastings in "The Perfect Crime".

The Tall Tales of Tommy Kenyon

According to Tommy Kenyon in "The Village That Wouldn't Talk", he had made arrangements to meet Jim Dawson at the Edisford Bridge Hotel on the night of March 18th 1934. Kenyon says that he subsequently changed his mind about meeting Jim and instead decided to go to the Red Pump in Bashall Eaves, where he met up with two or three mates. Kenyon and his companions left the Red Pump and arrived in the vicinity of the murder scene by car just before 9.15 p.m. - very close to the time that the shooting took place. He then states quite categorically that as the car approached the entrance to Back Lane, he saw Jim Dawson in the car's headlights[*].

And here we have the first of many major problems. For not one of the initial statements taken by the police in 1934 from Tommy Kenyon, or the other four present in the car (Thomas Parker Allan and his fiancé, Frank Ireland and Billy Wright), make any mention whatsoever of having seen Jim Dawson illuminated in their headlights. Indeed Parker Allan stated that when they passed the place where Dawson was shot there was nobody around, and the only people they saw on the road were a man and woman with a dog. No mention of Jim Dawson.

What are we to make of this? One thing is for sure - if any of the passengers in Parker Allan's car did see Jim in the headlights that night, they certainly did not tell the police about it in 1934. I was unfortunately unable to trace the statement of the driver of the second car by whose headlights Jim spotted the lurking figure at the Brieryforth gate. It would have been interesting to see if he had claimed to have seen Jim that night. I suspect that he did not, otherwise this important evidence placing Jim Dawson at the murder scene at 9.15 p.m. would surely have been mentioned at the Inquest.

Kenyon further stated in 1979 that after seeing Jim, the car just carried on to Clitheroe, whereas all the statements in 1934 agree that the car actually slowed right down at the top of Back Lane to drop Kenyon off, but that he suddenly changed his mind (again) and decided to accompany his friends to the Swan and Royal Hotel in Clitheroe.

He further claims to have arrived back home at Bashall Hall at 11.00 p.m., and found Jim sitting up in a chair. Jim even asked him a question, *"Hast thou been to Edisford Bridge tonight?"* Yet in 1934 Kenyon stated to the police that when he arrived home at 10.30 p.m., everyone was in bed. And this agrees with all the statements given by Jim's family at the time.

By 1979, Kenyon could not even remember who was actually present at Bashall Hall on the night of March 18th, 1934. When asked by Barry Shaw who else was in the house, he listed Lily, Polly, Annie and Albert Pickles. Lily Lee, along with Polly Pickles and her son Albert were certainly there. Annie Dawson, however, was not. She was sleeping elsewhere that night. And Tommy Kenyon appeared to have forgotten the very existence of my father, Jack Lee, who was upstairs in the same bedroom as the victim, Jim Dawson!

---

[*] In 1980, Kenyon told us that he did not see Jim Dawson in the headlights because he was not in the front seat, but one of his companions saw him and said to Kenyon, "Your boss is here, Tommy!"

Barry Shaw then proceeded to embellish Kenyon's erroneous evidence (i.e. that Jim Dawson was still up at 11 p.m., which he certainly was not) in order to suggest that Jim may have got up after the rest of the family had gone to bed. He could therefore have been shot at another time and in another place, maybe in the small hours of the night. Once again, over the years this hypothesis has gained credence with many locals, who seem blissfully unaware that the theory originated from a television programme and was based upon a serious factual error. Local memory was thus further contaminated.

On the morning after the shooting, Barry Shaw stated that Tommy Kenyon had seen one of the sisters mopping up blood from round the hearth in the kitchen. He also stated that there was blood on the chair Jim had been sitting in. To clear up the mistaken idea that there was blood all over the place once and for all, it should be reiterated that there were three tiny spots of blood at the top of the stairs, and blood both in and beneath Jim's bed. There was no trace of any blood downstairs whatsoever.

The television programme then got down to the nitty-gritty, and Kenyon was encouraged to speculate about possible motives and suspects. Barry Shaw suggested to him that Chief Superintendent Blacker had grave doubts about Albert Pickles, Jim Dawson's nephew. Kenyon, while stating that he did not think Albert had done it, agreed with Shaw that Albert had changed a lot after the murder. Not only that, but he 'went drinking' and died soon after. The truth of it is that Albert Pickles did not change after the murder, drank no more after the murder than he did before it took place, and died in 1952, which can hardly be described as 'soon after'.

The next and indeed the prime suspect on the hit list was, however, Tommy Simpson of Bashall Town Farm. We are informed that Simpson had three children (in fact he had four) and that he was a widely respected and liked figure in the local community. Barry Shaw swiftly sows the seeds of suspicion about Simpson in the viewer's mind by asserting that when the police searched his land, they found something very strange...This turned out to be the dog which had been shot, and subsequently exhumed by the police and X-rayed. According to the newspaper report at the time, there was a large wound in the dog, but no sign of any large bullet, or any exit wound, thus implying that the bullet had been removed for further use after testing out its efficacy on the animal.

Shaw states that he found the information about the dog in a small paragraph in the local Clitheroe newspaper. Had Shaw (or his researchers) read the paragraph with a little more care, he would have seen that the Clitheroe Advertiser and Times stated quite clearly that the dog was found at Bashall Hall, and the Simpson land (i.e. Bashall Town) is nowhere mentioned in the story. While we have already seen that the tale of the shot dog is certainly a strange and rather sinister one, it had nothing whatsoever to do with Tommy Simpson. He simply didn't come into it.

Kenyon went on to describe his turbulent relationship with Simpson, culminating in the brawl at Bashall Town described earlier. He also talked at length about Nancy Simpson, "*She were a fit lass. She were that.*" He stated that he thought Simpson had mistakenly got it into his head that he, Kenyon, was the father of Nancy's illegitimate child Jimmy*, and that he was therefore the man who was meant to be murdered that night. The home-made steel bullet made by Tommy Simpson to kill Kenyon that night had been fired at Jim Dawson in error.

To add credence to the idea that Tommy Simpson was the murderer, Kenyon informed the television presenter that Simpson's nephew and farmhand, Henry Bleazard, had told him something which he had until that moment kept to himself. Kenyon disclosed to the reporter that Henry Bleazard had told him his uncle Tommy Simpson had secretly carried a sack from Bashall Town to Whalley Nab. When asked what Kenyon thought was in the sack he replied, *"Well, the gun and part of poker that were left."* He claimed he had not told the police about this at the time because they did not ask him.

Now this was pure trouble-making. As we have seen, the police had no need of Kenyon's assistance in this matter, as they had recovered the items smuggled out from Bashall Town as a result of intelligence gained from 24-hour surveillance of the Simpson property. And the gun in question had turned out to be nothing whatsoever to do with the murder. In 1979, Kenyon gave the impression that he was imparting new and secret evidence to the television people which implicated Tommy Simpson in the murder of Jim Dawson. It is also implied that the police never had access to this information in 1934.

What I personally find curious about Kenyon's story, however, is his remark about the contents of the sack - he thought the smuggled bag contained *the gun and part of poker that were left.* Presumably he was intending to imply that the home-made bullet had been manufactured from the tip of a fire poker. This is the only mention of such a scenario. Nobody mentioned pokers in 1934. A steel rod, yes, but never a poker.

---

* Both Kenyon and Nancy Simpson made it clear in the programme that Kenyon was not the father of her illegitimate child. Shaw suggested to Nancy that local people had told him that Jim Dawson was the father. This Nancy utterly denied, saying it was nothing to do with Jim, who was much older than she was.

Bashall Town, the home of the Simpson family in 1934.
Photo: N. J. Cobban

Tommy Simpson's suicide

The final misleading piece of evidence submitted in support of the theory that Tommy Simpson shot Jim Dawson by mistake was even more pernicious. Kenyon stated that something had been preying on Simpson's mind and as a result he hanged himself about a week or ten days after the murder, the implication being, of course, that he could not live with what he had done to his friend Jim.

Tommy Simpson did indeed commit suicide by hanging himself from a beam in the loft in Bashall Town's barn[*], but this happened on June 22nd, 1936 - a couple of **years** after the murder of Jim Dawson took place, not a couple of weeks. The producer of "The Village That Wouldn't Talk" admitted the mistake soon after. By this time, however, it was too late. The programme had already been aired and the long-term damage to Simpson's reputation had already been done. In 1987, for example, the Lancashire Evening Telegraph stated, *"The most popular theory locally is that Jim Dawson was killed by another farm labourer, Tommy Simpson, who hanged himself shortly after the death."*

Things are no different today. I have been informed by some local people that Simpson must have had something to hide because he committed suicide a week or so after the murder. When I tell them gently that this was a mistake made in a television programme and that Tommy Simpson killed himself two years later, I am advised in a condescending manner that it is I who am mistaken. This patronising attitude has been encountered more than once during the course of my research into the murder of my great-uncle, and has regularly left me fighting the temptation to gnaw my own arm off.

Tommy Kenyon's inaccurate statements in "The Village That Wouldn't Talk" concerning Tommy Simpson's suicide have thus seeped insidiously into local memory and consciousness, and are now proving extremely difficult to dislodge.

Apart from the timing of Tommy Simpson's suicide, there is also the question of his reasons for killing himself. All the evidence points to his suicide being the result of a combination of unfortunate and stressful circumstances.

His widow Kate stated at the Inquest, which was held at Bashall Town and was attended by Superintendent Elliott, *"He had been very grieved about being summoned recently about the milk, and also because the case was not finished; it should have been heard again at Manchester on Tuesday."*

She went on to say that her husband had also been worrying about financial matters generally and had said that his head was bad from all the worrying about the quality of the milk. On top of all this, he was suffering from a rupture which had been upsetting him very much. He should have gone to Blackburn Infirmary for treatment, but had kept putting it off. It is also possible that he had never fully recovered from the stress he had suffered during the police enquiry into Jim's death two years earlier.

---

[*] The site of the present café at Bashall Barn.

The wedding of Nancy Simpson in 1935. Henry Bleazard, whose gun was mysteriously smuggled out of Bashall Town in 1934, is standing second from the left. Seated in front of him is Nancy's sister, Kathleen. Fifth from the left, Thomas Dewhurst stands next to his bride Nancy. On Nancy's right stand her parents, Tommy Simpson (who hanged himself in 1936) and his wife Kate. Nancy's brothers Richard and Cyril are for some reason absent.
Photo: family archive

Tommy Simpson left a suicide note in his wife's handbag. The contents were not divulged at the Inquest, but we can be pretty sure that Superintendent Elliott read the letter and that it therefore contained no reference to the murder of Jim Dawson. Had Simpson been responsible for Jim's murder, he would surely have got it off his chest before he died.

The unwarranted attack on an old family friend in "The Village That Wouldn't Talk" goaded my father Jack Lee into the unprecedented action of contacting the local newspapers, albeit anonymously, to object to the 'very wild theories expounded by Tom Kenyon' in the programme.

Jack has always regarded the media with deep mistrust. This attitude may well stem from the reporting methods employed by journalists at the time of his Uncle Jim's murder. The first story about the murder which appeared in the Clitheroe Advertiser and Times on 23rd March 1934 contained a long statement supposedly made by Jack's mother, Lily Lee. This puzzled both Jack and his mother when they read it, because together they had told two reporters at the door of Bashall Hall to go away in no uncertain terms. Lily Lee had made no statement of any kind to them. Since this time, Jack had refused to have anything to do with the media in any shape or form.

It is therefore a measure of his exasperation that he broke the habit of a lifetime, and contacted the newspapers with his opinion of the latest television programme.

He was particularly scathing about the 'mistaken identity' theory put forward in the programme, *"There is no possibility that Jim Dawson could have been mistaken for Tom Kenyon himself - as suggested in the programme - because Jim's very ordinary brisk walk was very dissimilar to Tom Kenyon's distinctive rolling gait. Tommy Simpson had known both men for many years and could not have mistaken one for the other. Indeed, I and others who knew both men could have told the difference between the sounds of the two men's walks even in pitch black conditions...At no time was Tommy Simpson entered in my personal list of possible suspects or on the suspect list of my family and this firm opinion still holds today."*

So let it be said once and for all - the police could find no evidence whatsoever to connect Tommy Simpson with the murder of Jim Dawson in 1934 and no reliable evidence to suggest that he was involved has come to light since that time.

* * * * * * * * *

As we can see, therefore, theories abound concerning the mysterious and unsolved murder of Jim Dawson at Bashall Eaves in March 1934. Jim could have been shot completely by accident, or as the result of jealousy arising from clandestine love affair or even as a result of mistaken identity. The mystery murder weapon may have been a conventional firearm (if Jim had been shot by accident from some distance away), or it could have been an air cane or even a catapult. All theorists struggle to explain both the 'click' which Jim heard just before he was hit, and reasons for the murderer having manufactured a large home-made bullet. Finally they have strained to come up with a potential identity for the murderer.

While all these ideas are interesting and thought-provoking, some are, as we have seen, based upon inaccurate information and faulty memory. They must, for that reason, be treated with extreme caution.

The aim of this book has always been to present as full a picture as possible of my personal research into the murder of my great-uncle. Moving back to the Clitheroe area in 2002 finally gave me the opportunity to delve far more deeply into his case than had hitherto proved possible. I hoped that, after 70 years, the supposed 'wall of silence' might have developed a few chinks through which, as a member of Jim Dawson's family, I might be able to winkle out a few new snippets of information. It was now time to do a little local digging and cajoling.

Additionally, while appreciating that the chance of any clue having been overlooked was negligible, I began to sift through all the evidence again with a fine tooth comb. Could the police possibly have missed anything during the 1934 murder investigation? And might they perhaps have placed too much faith in the advice of their gun expert, Robert Churchill?

CHAPTER 8

Final thoughts, a hidden gun and a deathbed confession(?)

WHILE nobody could argue that certain aspects of this unsolved murder case are extremely puzzling, some of the mysteries surrounding the case of Jim Dawson seem to have arisen from a combination of ignorance of his character and a general failure to take into consideration the historical circumstances in which he found himself. An examination of Jim's personal history together with analysis of documents relating to the murder soon provided credible explanations for a few of the minor mysteries associated with the case.

Minor mysteries

At the time of the investigation, the police officers appear to have had great difficulty in believing that Jim could have walked from Back Lane to Bashall Hall (a distance of just under half a mile) with a large bullet lodged in his shoulder. This initial scepticism has been exploited by more recent studies into the case, even leading to suggestions that Jim's police statement was a fabrication. In reality, it is argued, he must have been shot at another time and in another location.

In fact, Jim's ability to walk to Bashall Hall after he had been shot is really no mystery at all. As was made quite clear at the Inquest in June 1934, many veterans of The Great War managed to stay on their feet after being wounded in battle. Dr. Gilbert Bailey, the police surgeon, provided evidence that he had personally managed to walk a couple of miles after being shot during the war and commented, *"Most people think it is incredible to have a bullet in you and not realise that you are badly hurt but it is quite possible."*

People have also tried to weave mysteries around Jim's behaviour and attitude in the aftermath of the shooting. They find it hard to understand why, after he returned home to Bashall Hall that evening, he told nobody what had just happened in Back Lane. They find it even harder to understand why he failed to raise the household during the night when in a great deal of pain and distress. There are several possible reasons for this behaviour. We have already seen that waking everybody up just wasn't Jim's style. He would have seen it as making an unnecessary fuss.

But apart from this we also have to take into consideration the fact that Jim Dawson was in all probability severely shocked by the previous night's attack. The question of how the trauma of being shot affected Jim physically and psychologically has never really been addressed. As he was in all likelihood already suffering from post traumatic stress disorder as a result of his experiences in The Great War, this previous history of trauma must surely, therefore, have increased the risk of serious symptoms in March 1934.

We must therefore take into consideration the idea that Jim's entire attitude to the shooting may well have been clouded by the symptoms of severe shock.

We have seen for example that, on the morning following the incident, his sisters were surprised that he did not seem to be unduly worried by the realisation that somebody had shot him the night before. While this reaction may partly be explained by Jim's quiet character, we also have to remember that a feeling of inappropriate calmness can be a symptom of trauma.

Much speculation has also arisen as a result of Jim's refusal to have the bullet removed on 19th March. As we have seen, this may have been due to the cost of the operation, or fear of the operation itself. Also, Jim may have thought surgery a more dangerous option than keeping the bullet inside him, especially as he had kidney problems. But there is the additional possibility that he was in denial about the whole incident, and was attempting to shrug it off, for another symptom of trauma is the effort to avoid any thoughts of the cause of the traumatic event.

Victims of serious crime are often unwilling to co-operate fully with the police, because this requires them to 're-live' the event and is a result not of apathy but of fear. There is the distinct possibility therefore that Jim was not thinking straight when Inspector Elliott interviewed him and took him down to the scene of the incident the day after it had taken place. While Jim seems to have produced a reasonably full account of his walk home from the Edisford Bridge Hotel, it is very possible that delayed shock may have rendered him physically incapable of recalling that night's events with complete accuracy. A vital piece of evidence could even have slipped his mind completely.

Both the West Riding Constabulary and the family gained the impression at the time that Jim knew more about the assault than he had told the police. Possibly he did, and possibly he did not. But it is worth bearing in mind that his behaviour, and apparent refusal to say any more than he did, may well have been the result of trauma rather than any desire on his part to keep any part of the incident secret. It is entirely possible that Jim Dawson was telling the truth when he asserted he had no idea who had shot him.

Rational explanations for some of the minor puzzles arising from Jim Dawson's apparently mysterious behaviour after the shooting can therefore be offered for consideration. However, other mysteries remain for which it is far from easy to suggest solutions. These are, of course, the weapon, the home-made bullet and the motivation behind the attack - not to mention the identity of the assailant and how he endeavoured to shoot Jim on such a dark night unless he was within a couple of yards of his victim.

I originally hoped that the post-mortem report might throw a little light on the latter question as I understand that it is often possible to deduce from the shape of a bullet entry wound the approximate distance (i.e. point blank, intermediate or long range) from which a victim has been shot. Unfortunately, however, the report indicated that a surgical incision had been made at the site of the entry wound in order to remove the bullet. Dr. Gilbert Bailey, the police surgeon, therefore had no opportunity to comment upon the shape of the wound as it had already been destroyed by the surgeon's knife at the Blackburn nursing home. This is a pity.

Some information about the direction from which Jim was shot might these days perhaps be gleaned from the X-ray of Jim's back taken on 19th March 1934 – if we knew where it was, that it. Additionally, scientific analysis of his clothes could conceivably throw a little light on Jim's activities in the last few hours of his life. But, of course, the whereabouts of the bundle of clothes handed over to P.C. Sheldon on 19th March is also a mystery. Any attempt at a fresh examination of the case would always be frustrated by missing evidence.

Thoughts on the home-made bullet

Was it possible to obtain any fresh information about the murder weapon, the home-made bullet or the mysterious click which Jim heard? I was beginning to doubt it; indeed the more I looked into these aspects of the case, the more questions seemed to present themselves. The bullet is today a puzzle in its own right. Its very size and shape now seem to be uncertain as this detail was not recorded at the Inquest, and I found no measurements or photographs of the bullet in the case file at Newby Wiske. The newspapers at the time described the bullet as 'like a bird's egg' while Lily Lee compared it to a dum-dum bullet.

The only written dimensions of the bullet I have been able to find are recorded in Macdonald Hastings' "The Other Mr. Churchill" (1963). He states that it was half an inch long and the same in diameter (.500 calibre) therefore suggesting to me that the object must have been almost circular (or indeed egg-shaped). Hastings then proceeded to confuse matters in his programme "The Perfect Crime" a year later by holding up to the viewer a bullet of a conventional shape, much longer than it was wide, and claiming that this was the actual bullet which had killed Jim Dawson. As we have seen, however, fact and fiction freely intermingled in this programme, with no distinction being made between the two.

The post-mortem report makes it clear that the bullet must have been **less than** half an inch in diameter, as it states that *"the bullet wound in the muscle was less than half an inch in diameter"*. It stands to reason that the bullet could not have made a wound smaller than its own diameter. I can only deduce from all this that the bullet must have been oval in shape and of impressive size, but something less than .500 calibre. How much less is debatable, as there was talk at the Inquest of fitting it into a .410 cartridge.

We have already seen that Robert Churchill thought that the bullet must have been specially made to fit a particular barrel, but was at a loss to explain the 'click' which Jim Dawson heard just before he was struck. In an attempt to find an explanation, Macdonald Hastings came up with the idea of an air cane (the sizes of whose barrels were very variable, from .30 to .49 in calibre) as a likely candidate for the mystery gun that fired the home-made bullet. This weapon, when fired, makes a noise which Jim might conceivably have described as a click on a windy, wild night. In 1934, the police commented at the Inquest that a cane gun was an old fashioned weapon, of which they found no examples in their investigation.

However, it did set me thinking that everything always comes back to that blessed 'click' which Jim heard. While musing about it, a memory popped into my mind of sunny days in the 1960s, when I would go shooting with a friend who owned an airgun. This air rifle, I remembered, gave a sharp "click" when it was fired. Could the murder weapon have been an air rifle of some sort? These were less rare than air canes, though still very expensive items.

Was the weapon an air rifle?

There is a very interesting exchange at the Inquest between the Foreman of the Jury and Inspector Elliott on this very subject.

> The Foreman: Does it appear to be a possibility that the bullet was fired by an air gun?
>
> Superintendent Elliott: The bullet would not go through the barrel of an air gun.

The Jury Foreman seemed unconvinced and persisted:

> The Foreman: It could not have been done by a gun because there was no report. The catapult does make a click. There is no possibility of an air gun, is there?
>
> Superintendent Elliott: No. The only kind of air gun that would take this bullet would be a cane gun, which is out of date. We have made thorough inquiries in the district and have been unable to locate a single gun of that description.

So that was the Foreman of the Jury firmly put in his place. He was unlikely to argue further with an eminent police superintendent who was being advised by the foremost gun expert in the country. But he clearly wasn't convinced. And neither am I. For whatever Superintendent Elliott might have said, I believe that the bullet which killed Jim **could** have gone through the barrel of some airguns other than an air cane.

Airguns have been around for centuries, the first being seen in the sixteenth century, and these weapons only lost their popularity after the invention of cartridge bullets. Apart from their use in hunting, airguns were the early snipers' weapon of choice, because they were comparatively quiet when fired. It is said that they were employed by Austrian soldiers to demoralise Napoleon's troops in the late eighteenth century and became so feared that an enemy soldier captured by the French while in possession of an airgun was automatically executed on the spot as an assassin.

The nobility tried to ensure than poor people didn't get hold of them, because it was considered very easy to get away with crimes committed with these quiet weapons.

Airguns (of which air canes were but one example) were charged with pumps between 100 and 1000 times and were then good for up to 30 shots. From the late 1700s to the late 1800s, big bore shotguns were very popular with wealthy hunting folk. Air rifles, which came in big calibres from .30 to .51 calibres were also popular for hunting game.

One particular gun, which doubled as both shotgun and rifle, was made by Hass in Newstadt in Germany in about 1750. It had a 33" shot barrel, about .33 calibre. This could be unscrewed and removed to reveal a .46 calibre barrel. Another example, an English air rifle made in about 1850, fired a .44 calibre bullet.

Yet Superintendent Elliott, at Jim Dawson's Inquest, told the jury that the home-made bullet in question would not fit into the barrel of an airgun. These came in such widely varying barrel sizes that this seems a nonsense. The police seem to have refused to consider the possibility of an old weapon having been utilized in the shooting of Jim Dawson.

As we have seen, Elliott commented that the only airgun barrel that the bullet would fit would be that of an cane gun, but this was out-of-date. It is hard to see why the murderer should have been particularly concerned about being fashionable in his weapon of choice. Superintendent Elliott also stated that not a single example of such a weapon came to light during the police searches. Well, it wouldn't, would it, if the murderer had hidden it well! And it is a fact that air canes were still in use in the area in 1934, as Jim's old school friend Bill Eccles told us in 1980.

However, it would seem that we are not limited to air canes as far as potential weapons go in any case, because there were other types of old (and probably more common) air guns which could have fired the large home-made bullet. There was nothing whatsoever to prevent a farmer being in possession of an old air rifle lying around in his collection in 1934, for most farmers had several guns on their premises and it is unlikely that many were ever actually thrown away. Some may even have owned old hunting air rifles, for we are in the Forest of Bowland where shooting parties had been a country pastime for centuries. We can also consider the possibility that an antique foreign weapon may have been collected abroad by a farmer during his service in The Great War. However, it would be difficult to obtain ammunition for any of these out-of-date guns - thus explaining the necessity of manufacturing a home-made bullet.

But why choose an old air gun to carry out the assault on Jim Dawson? Why not just use an ordinary firearm? The answer perhaps lies in the relative silence of airguns. The noise made by an air rifle would attract far less attention from passers-by than the loud bang of a firearm. Indeed, most passers-by would hear absolutely nothing, especially on such a wild night.

I find it difficult to understand why Elliott and Churchill did not consider antique air guns more seriously during the investigation, especially as Robert Churchill had commented that the only reason he could think of for manufacturing a home-made bullet would be to use it in an obsolete weapon. It is very strange. The Foreman of the Jury at the Inquest obviously thought so too.

We are still left with the problem of how the assailant managed to see Jim 30 yards up Back Lane from the Brieryforth gate. As I have already mentioned, this would surely have been impossible, and the assailant must have crept up close behind Jim in order to be able to see him. I can think of only one possible way Jim could have been seen from further away on such a dark night, and even I am not particularly convinced by my own idea. However, there is nothing lost in recording it.

The last thing Jim Dawson did before he left the Edisford Bridge Hotel was to buy a box of matches. It therefore occurred to me that he might have walked home smoking his pipe and that the murderer could see where he was by the glow of his pipe as he pulled on it.

I doubted, however, that it was actually feasible to keep a pipe alight on a windy and wet night, but a pipe smoker whom I consulted considers it feasible. However, he also made the point that he did not consider a pipe capable of producing enough of a glow to enable Jim to be seen from so far away. Perhaps the only way to settle this would be to carry out an experiment with a pipe on a dark and windy night on Back Lane.

Hiding places

As we have seen, no examples of air canes turned up in the 'very wide search' made by the police, and at this point we have to ask ourselves just how thorough, in fact, these searches were. In the initial hunt for evidence, police searched 'hedges, ditches and pools over a wide area' in their vain quest to find the murder weapon. But I wonder if they investigated the two extremely deep wells located within half a mile of the shooting incident?

One of the wells, whose location is certainly still known today, is described in a publication called "The Rambler", (Volume 2) in 1906. Mr. Fielding, (whom we have met before when he and his ramblers gained access to Bashall Hall and complained about white paint smeared on the panelling) came across it during the course of one of his rambles in a field belonging to Thirty Acres Farm.

He described it thus, *"A few yards away, also, we mark a spot where a few large stones rest on some short planks that are seemingly rotting away. A close scrutiny discloses the reality of a hidden well beneath the planks. This is said to be of great depth, and well-constructed, being faced with stone to its utmost depth. This is supposed to have supplied the inmates of the place* [Edisford Leper Hospital] *with water and we have no doubt it would give forth a most bountiful supply at the present time."* He went on to say, *"We often wonder why some interested owners do not formulate a scheme of excavation which would either destroy such conjectures or confirm them."*

It would indeed be interesting to investigate both the construction and the contents of this well. It is quite probable that the police were unaware of its presence in 1934. But the locals would have known about it.

Wells have always been handy places to dispose of unwanted or incriminating bits and pieces and the example at Thirty Acres is not an isolated example in the area. Another well is marked on old maps at Cheetall Farm, which again is only half a mile or so from the scene of the crime. No doubt there were others in the vicinity, for example at Brieryforth Farm.

And just how thoroughly did the police investigate buildings in the Clitheroe and Bashall Eaves area? We know that they went to the trouble of ferreting underneath Tommy Simpson's carpets, of course, but was every farm building in the neighbourhood subjected to such a rigorous search? This seems very unlikely, for it would have been a mammoth task to explore each nook and cranny of every farmhouse, barn and outbuilding in the area. Without a motive or a suspect, it would have been difficult for the police to justify particular targets for exhaustive searches. It was like looking for the proverbial needle in a haystack. And as we have mentioned before, the assailant or assailants had already gained four days' grace to conceal the weapon before the murder investigation proper had even got underway. It is hardly surprising, therefore, that the police never found the mystery murder weapon.

The Clitheroe Advertiser and Times commented on August 14th 1964 in the aftermath of Macdonald Hastings', The Perfect Crime, *"As the television programme pointed out, somewhere in some attic or cellar may be lying the strange weapon which fired the carefully-tooled bullet, and inside the barrel, although it is so many years since it was used, will be the scratch marks made by the bullet."*.

This sounded a little on the melodramatic and unlikely side. Or so I thought until a few years ago, when rumours began to filter through to the family of the discovery of a 'funny-looking gun' in a barn near the Edisford Bridge Hotel, where Jim Dawson had been drinking on the night of the shooting.

The Hidden Gun

I first became aware of this interesting and potentially vital discovery in the mid-1990s. However, being in London at that time meant that I could not seek further information in person. I therefore asked my father, Jack Lee, to visit the locality concerned to see what he could find out. On 26th November 1997, he 'phoned me with interesting news. The owners of the building in question had confirmed to him that a hidden gun had indeed been discovered in the barn some ten years earlier. It had come to light resting on the top of a high beam when re-slating work was being carried out to the roof. Contrary to our original information, the owner maintained that it was an ordinary gun, but gave no further details. When asked about the present whereabouts of the weapon, the owner claimed that the family gave it away shortly after it had been found, and that she could not remember to whom they had given it. She seemed generally reluctant to discuss the matter.

Although I was far from content with the story which had been given to my father, there matters had to rest for several years until I was in a position to make enquiries for myself. After six years of fuming frustration I eventually managed to pay an unannounced visit to the site on April 30th 2003, dragging my unwilling father along with me. I wanted to hear this peculiar tale for myself and I wanted a witness to be present.

When we arrived at the premises near the Edisford Bridge Hotel at 9.35 a.m. we found the front door of the cottage open and a man preparing tiles just outside. I enquired of him if a member of the family was at home. The man went indoors and quickly appeared with the lady of the house. Having introduced myself and my father, I informed her that I was investigating the shooting and murder of my great-uncle Jim Dawson in 1934 with the intention of writing a book about the case. I told her that I understood they had found a gun concealed on their property, and asked for further details as it could very well be connected to the case, as the murder weapon was never found.

The lady confirmed to me that they had found a gun concealed on their property some years previously. I eagerly requested more details, the main question being of course the gun's location, as I wished to examine it. At that, she said she would have to talk to someone, and disappeared into the house for three or four minutes.

When she re-appeared, I rapidly found myself embroiled in what is, without question, one of the most confusing and irritating conversations of my entire life. The lady told me that the gun had been found on the top of a beam in the barn during roof work, and that a relative had subsequently given it away. It transpired that this relative had allegedly given it to a member of the ambulance service who was also a gun collector. When I attempted to discover more about the gun's appearance things became very confused. The lady said she had never seen it because she was not interested in guns, although they had several on the property, all safely under lock and key. I found it difficult to credit that she could know nothing about the gun's appearance and persisted with my question. She said that it was a rifle type.

"So", I asked, "just an ordinary rifle, then?"

"Not a usual sort of gun," came her reply. This was becoming more impenetrable by the second. Feeling I was getting nowhere here, I attempted to return to the question of why the gun had been given away to someone and why the discovery of a concealed firearm had not been reported to the authorities. The reply was perplexing to say the least. I was told that they thought it might have something to do with some old shooting that happened in the area years ago. This seemed a strange thing to say, bearing in mind who we were and why we were there. I told her for the second time that we were the great-niece and the nephew of the victim of that shooting incident, and that was why we were asking her about the gun in the first place. However, it had become obvious to me that no straight answers would be forthcoming and indeed that proved to be the case. I had got no further than my father had done six years earlier.

Having reiterated that the gun they had found might well be a vital piece of evidence in a murder case, I handed her my 'phone number in case her family changed its mind and decided to give us some helpful information in the future regarding the present whereabouts of the weapon. I also thought it only fair to inform her that I intended to include the discovery of the gun on their property in the forthcoming book. As we turned to go, she made the comment that she could not understand how we had found out about it in the first place. Well, we have our ways and means.

Since the visit took place, I have checked the original information with our initial informant, who verified that the weapon found was actually seen by the informant's sister, and that it was most definitely a 'funny-looking' gun. It seems at least possible, therefore, that it might have been an antique air rifle of some description, or even an air cane. Unfortunately, the person who actually saw the weapon has since died and no further information from the finders has ever been received.

After 70 years, it seems that the case of Jim Dawson continues to generate inexplicable and bizarre puzzles. I remain extremely perplexed by the whole situation surrounding the discovery of the hidden gun. Surely if you find a strange-looking gun secreted on your property, and you know that an unsolved murder had taken place in the vicinity for which the murder weapon was never found, the sensible course of action is to inform the authorities of the discovery - especially as the murder victim had been drinking in the pub a few yards away, only minutes before he was shot. Yet rather than inform the police or the newspapers, the gun is instead allegedly handed over to a relative stranger, and its discovery kept quiet **because** it may have had something to do with an old shooting incident. This sort of back-to-front reasoning is enough to make your head spin right off its neck. The failure to report such a thing as a hidden gun seems to provide yet more fuel for the continuing speculation about the negative and secretive character of the area. It also leads me to the inescapable conclusion that if the same attitude prevailed among the farming community back in 1934, the West Riding Constabulary never had a hope in hell of solving the murder of Jim Dawson.

However, while I would dearly like to see this gun one day, we should always keep in mind that it would be impossible to connect it scientifically with the death of Jim Dawson even if it were brought forward. Should the gun's barrel be marked with bullet scratches, this would be interesting but that is all. As the bullet itself has vanished, there would be no way of matching it to this weapon. Fate seems to conspire against any progress being made towards a solution of this cold case mystery.

Neither is it reasonable to jump to conclusions about the identity of the murderer by working out who owned, or rented this Edisford property in 1934. Presumably quite a few people had access to the barn in question, and it is unlikely that it was locked up during the night.

We should also bear in mind that even if the gun was indeed concealed at Edisford in March 1934 this does not **automatically** indicate that it was utilized in the murder of Jim Dawson. We have seen that, although it had no relevance to the murder, Tommy Simpson smuggled his nephew's gun out of Bashall Town Farm and attempted to hide it with relatives in Billington. Equally, the Edisford gun may have been concealed not because it was the murder weapon, but because it was a weapon which the owner did not wish the police to find by chance during the murder enquiry. It might, for example, have been stolen. Gun theft appears to have been quite a common offence at the time. There is also the possibility that the gun might have been hidden at Edisford at another time entirely.

However having said all that (in the interests of historical 'good practice') this intriguing discovery of a 'funny looking' hidden gun at Edisford remains the most interesting piece of potential new evidence to come to light for many years and in my opinion might well be the mysterious murder weapon for which the police sought after in vain back in 1934. It strikes me as rather a coincidence, to say the least, that a gun should be found hidden in a barn close to the pub where Jim Dawson spent his last few hours before being shot. From the vague description available, the gun just might be an old fashioned air rifle or air cane, or possibly an antique firearm of some sort. And the fact that it was never retrieved by the owner but left in position on the top of the beam might perhaps be an indication that it had played a part in a serious crime.

Unfortunately, having once come to light the gun has now, to all intents and purposes, gone and concealed itself again . . . Should the "ambulance-driver-cum-gun-collector" (if he ever existed) happen to be reading, he would earn my undying gratitude if he came forward with the weapon to enable its official identification and documentation.

Strange attitudes, interesting letters and anonymous phone calls

I had very much hoped that being 'on the spot' in the Clitheroe area after so many years would lead to me obtaining some interesting new information where others had failed. What I had not bargained for, however, was this truly peculiar attitude towards the murder still persisting in the neighbourhood after nearly three quarters of a century. Upon being questioned about the case, most people will smile meaningfully and intone, *"Everybody knows who did it but nobody said"* like it was some weird sort of local mantra or spell. Some people (quite innocently) offered me theories which I had already seen on television, which made no sense whatsoever having seen the original police evidence. In one instance, a man advised me that he had been informed of the identity of the murderer some years previously by a couple of people independently, but no amount of wheedling could bring forth an actual name. It was all very tiresome.

I began to arrive at the reluctant conclusion that the murder of my great-uncle Jim Dawson had turned into a local sport - titles for which might include "mystify the media" "fox the family" and "stump the stranger". It was almost as if some people (certainly not all) in the area, while complaining publicly about their portrayal in "The Perfect Crime" and "The Village That Wouldn't Talk" had in reality come to enjoy and embrace this very reputation and were now playing up to it for all they were worth. I also began to suspect that I was becoming embroiled in mind games and that nobody was really interested any longer in the truth of what really happened back in 1934.

After so many years, Jim had ceased to be a flesh and blood person who had suffered horrible pain at the hands of a murderer. He had been reduced to the faceless focus of a baffling and bizarre murder mystery and that was how people preferred to keep it.

This attitude, combined with the contamination of local memory meant that I was now very doubtful of being able to throw much new light on the murder of my great uncle. Yet I could not rid myself of the notion that there might be somebody out there who had hitherto stayed out of 'the game' and who just might hold the key to the mystery.

With this in mind as the 70th anniversary of Jim's murder approached in March 2004, I resolved to make a final public plea for genuine information in the local newspapers, ending the letter with the words, *"Since returning recently to live in the area, I have been somewhat irritated (and to be honest, rather sceptical) to be told repeatedly that 'everybody knew who did it but nobody said anything'. I would now, therefore, appeal to anyone who thinks they know anything whatsoever about this 'cold case' to reveal that information once and for all and have done with it (even if they think a member of my own family may have been responsible). It will prove interesting to see if anybody really does have a credible theory concerning the identity of the killer - or merely thinks that they have. Any information will be most gratefully received."*

The Clitheroe Advertiser and Times printed the letter on 18th March under the delightful headline, **"My uncle's murder - tell me who did it!"**. (Or else, it seemed to imply.) The Lancashire Evening Telegraph had even more fun with their headline on March 19th when it ran a piece entitled, **"End this wall of silence : Author calls to blow lid off killing"**.

The newspaper appeal produced some nice background details about the case. I was delighted to receive a letter from Mr. J. S. Bailey of Clitheroe, who turned out to be the son of Dr. Gilbert Bailey, the police surgeon who had carried out the post-mortem on Jim's body. The letter contained the interesting point that, *"In the early 1960s my father was approached by the BBC on his version of the case as they wanted to incorporate it in a Z Cars episode."* This was fascinating. For those too young to remember, Z Cars was a twice-weekly police drama, and was aired from January 1962 until September 1978. It was an extremely popular series, whose title referred to the Ford Zephyr cars which the police used as patrol vehicles in the fictional provincial town of Newtown. Unfortunately only half the episodes survive today, and I have been unable to establish whether or not Jim Dawson's murder was ever used as a basis for one of its plots.

I was also touched to receive a letter from a Mrs. Gertrude Hird in Devon, whose grandparents had once farmed Mason Green Farm in Bashall Eaves. She said, *"I was just a child, but I remember vividly my mother, Maggie Peel, feeling very sad about Jim Dawson who she had known very well. He was a nice chap, I gather, and it was such a tragedy."*

A Deathbed Confession?

As well as these kind letters, I also received some anonymous 'phone calls. One of these informed me that 'the way the Bashall Eaves murder works' is that the secret of who murdered Jim Dawson is passed on through family generations to the present day by a series of deathbed confessions. The caller suggested that I speak to a local who would give me further information.

This idea of deathbed confessions also surfaces on a local radio web page on which a local tour guide can be seen telling the story of the Jim Dawson murder - much of which is inaccurate. I was not encouraged therefore to lend much credence to this 'phone call, because as usual it was tricky to determine whether the person who called me was offering genuine new information about the murder or was innocently repeating a modern fabrication as fact.

However, having appealed to the general public for information it was necessary to chase down every clue and this one was followed up immediately in spite of serious reservations.

Regrettably, although I was offered an interesting motive for the crime - that it had happened because Jim Dawson and his alleged murderer had both been pursuing Nancy Simpson - the actual evidence that a deathbed confession had ever taken place was unsatisfactory. Vague second-hand assertions from unknown people made through a third party will not do at all. For it to be convincing evidence, it would be necessary to hear testaments directly from the mouths of the actual people who were present when the dying man confessed to the murder of Jim Dawson. And they would have to be very reliable witnesses with no axe to grind. Until such witnesses come forward, the deathbed confession of the murderer must therefore remain yet another unsubstantiated local rumour.

March 2004 had one last surprise up its sleeve in the form of a particularly silly episode. This involved (as far as I could make out) a man claiming to be Jim Dawson's son turning up on the doorstep of somebody I knew slightly. This acquaintance would not give me the name of the man concerned. (No surprise there, then.) Having mentioned genetic testing, nothing further was heard about 'Jim Dawson's son'.

As a result of my appeal for information in the local papers, BBC North West's "Inside Out" spent three days in the Bashall Eaves area in July 2004 filming a ten minute piece about my quest to discover the truth about Jim Dawson's murder. The filming was great fun; apart from the moment when I toppled off a bar stool in the Edisford Bridge Hotel in the middle of a serious conversation with crime expert Vincent Burke. I wasn't drunk. The bar stool was too high and it wobbled. That's my story and I'm sticking to it. The pub customers enjoyed it anyway, judging from the ripples of appreciative laughter.

Filming also took place at Back Lane and the Brieryforth gate as well as the graveyard at Mitton church and The Barracks at Bashall Hall. North Yorkshire Police also very kindly allowed the production team to film documents from the case file in Settle Police Station.

During a break in filming at Back Lane, Ken Ward, the camera man came up with an interesting suggestion for the murder weapon. He wondered if the 'click' Jim heard might have been made by a customised weapon of some sort involving the combination of a firearm barrel with a crossbow attachment to fire the bullet.

The programme was eventually broadcast on 11th October 2004 and provided a brief and colourful overview of the case. Full justice was done to the exquisite beauty of the countryside which, for once in this context, was permitted to look stunning rather than sinister.

* * * * * * * * *

The people of Bashall Eaves and the Clitheroe area have now been offered plenty of time and every opportunity to come forward with any previously suppressed information about the identity of the Jim Dawson's murderer. I would like to express thanks those who have come forward with facts of any kind. I hoped for an end to the 'cloak and dagger' approach, but this was not to be.

People with potentially new information preferred to remain anonymous, and have refused to name any names resulting in their testimony being reduced to the level of unsubstantiated local gossip. In many ways I can empathize with their attitude. People tend not to move away from the Clitheroe area. Many of those who do depart eventually seem, inexplicably, to be lured back to the beautiful valley under the watchful and protective eye of the mysterious and magical Pendle Hill. The surnames appearing in the electoral registers today differ very little from those of 1934. Practically every character involved in the dramatic events of March 1934 has descendants still living and working in the neighbourhood. People are therefore wary of saying too much and naming names, because a descendent of the person named might very well live just round the corner. Nothing much has changed here.

* * * * * * * * *

I have now endeavoured to record everything that I have discovered about the life and tragic death of Jim Dawson of Bashall Hall. Even at a time when the trail was relatively fresh, the case stumped those experienced detectives, Chief Superintendent Blacker and Superintendent Elliott of the West Riding Constabulary, not to mention Robert Churchill, the famous London gun expert. Having studied the case in minute detail for myself, I have to say that this does not surprise me in the slightest.

Apart from being a little more thorough in their search techniques, and perhaps employing a little more imagination when it came to the mystery murder weapon, I cannot see what more the police could have done under the circumstances. The investigating officers seem to have been particularly hampered and frustrated by one of the problems which I noted on examining the original witness statements. This was the nature of the alibis provided by most members of the farming community. Invariably these seemed to maintain that no members of the family had left the house on the night of 18th March 1934. Family members of such a tight-knit community were bound to support each other in this way and there was not much the police could do about it except note their frustration in their reports. It is therefore possible that certain people may have escaped being subjected to full investigation as they had witnesses willing and perhaps obliged to lie for them.

Albert Pickles, Jim Dawson's nephew, is a case in point as he had a typical alibi. He was at home all night. Initially, like Chief Superintendent Blacker, I did wonder about Albert and his catapult. However, this was before I had researched the family history and circumstances in any detail. It soon became obvious that Albert had no possible motive for killing his Uncle Jim and I had, in any case, soon reached the conclusion that a catapult was unlikely to be the murder weapon for reasons stated earlier. I am perfectly satisfied that none of my own family was responsible for the murder of Jim Dawson. Neither do I consider that there is any evidence that Tommy Simpson, the prime suspect at the time, was in any way involved. Of necessity I remain, on current evidence, rather sceptical about the alleged deathbed confession to the murder. Neither am I convinced that Jim was shot by accident or by a stranger.

Merrily disposing of potential suspects and theories left, right and centre is all very well, but the fact remains that **somebody** killed Jim Dawson, a man seemingly without an enemy in the world. In 90% of murder cases, the victim knows his murderer and it is quite possible, therefore, that somebody I have mentioned in passing could be the person responsible for his death. Alternatively, Jim may have had friends and acquaintances about which the family and the police knew nothing. But one thing I do believe is that Jim was acquainted with the person who shot him. Whether or not he saw and recognised his killer on that fateful night, and kept silent because the person was known to him is a conundrum to which the answer is unlikely to be forthcoming.

I consider that the mystery weapon used in Jim's murder is more than likely to have been an air rifle of some description and that the 'funny-looking' gun found near to the Edisford Bridge Hotel might very well have been hidden there by the murderer on the evening of 18th March 1934.

Obtaining a solution to "one of the greatest murder mysteries of the twentieth century" after 70 years was always going to prove problematic, and was never really the main objective of this particular study, which was to tell Jim Dawson's story as fully as possible and to reinstate his status as a man and a murder victim rather than a local myth. However, I freely admit that I did hope that in the course of my researches, I might come across a clue hitherto missed by previous investigators. Solving the mystery once and for all would have allowed Jim finally to rest in peace.

However, I hope that at the very least, some misconceptions about Jim Dawson and his family have finally been cleared up and that the detailed examination of the evidence will provide food for thought in any further studies of the case. As the Lancashire Evening Telegraph said on March 19th 2004, *"This is an examination of Jim's death rather than pointing the finger. It is up to the reader to deduce their findings."*

I will never rest in my own personal quest for the truth until the person responsible for the death of my great-uncle Jim Dawson is officially named and exposed as a murderer. Possibly this means I will never rest again until I join Uncle Jim in the next world. So be it. We will haunt Back Lane in Bashall Eaves together.

It only remains to record one final account of the murder which has been preserved within the family archives for 67 years. In 1938, four years after the murder of Jim Dawson had taken place and quite out of the blue, Little Mary, the clairvoyant, told Jim's relatives what had happened on the night of March 18th 1934. She insisted upon telling the family what she had 'seen' quite without warning and quite unbidden. This is what Little Mary had to say, and I record it without comment. Make of it what you will:

What the clairvoyant said

"Ten minutes before Jim Dawson left the pub, several people left including the person who eventually did the shooting.
He went to get his hidden gun and waited until Jim set off up the road to Bashall Hall. He then followed, not by the road, but alongside the road through the fields, eventually passing in order to arrive at the Brieryforth gate before Jim.
When Jim passed him he waited until Jim had gone up the side road a few yards and then shot - not to kill but to wound only.

The person who shot Jim Dawson was his best friend, and he will make a deathbed confession.
He shot Jim because he had been winning everything in sight, while he himself had won nothing."

APPENDIX 1

Diary of significant events in the life and death of Jim Dawson (1887 – 1934)

1887 - 1933

3 June 1887	Jim Dawson born at Bashall Hall.
23 April 1893	Jim Dawson joins Bashall Eaves Village School.
1895	Death of his mother Mary Dawson.
1897	Death of his father Matthew Dawson.
15 May 1897	Jim's uncle, Charles Dawson takes over Bashall Hall estate.

1903   Charles Dawson marries Isabella Parkinson.
Jim's brothers and sisters dissolve their partnership with Charles, and leave Bashall Hall for Colliers Farm, Billington.
Jim Dawson goes into farm service with his Uncle Charles at Bashall Hall.

1909   Jim Dawson leaves his uncle's employ and joins family at Colliers Farm, Billington.
William Dawson emigrates to Australia

1910   Felix Dawson emigrates to Australia
1912   Polly Dawson marries Albert Pickles, and has son Albert.
Death of Polly's husband.

1913   John, Jim and Harry Dawson go into partnership at Backridge Farm, Bashall Eaves.

1914   Outbreak of World War One.
Polly Pickles joins family at Backridge.
Bob Dawson joins Bedfordshire Regiment.

1915   Lily Dawson marries Charles Gordon Lee at Mitton church.
1916   Jim Dawson enlists in army and joins Lincolnshire Regiment.
Lily's son Jack Lee born.

1919   Charles Dawson dies at Bashall Hall.
John and Jim Dawson return to Bashall Hall with Polly as house and book keeper.

11 September	Peace celebrations take place at Bashall Eaves. Lee family leave Backridge for Birkenhead. Jim Dawson has a breakdown and begins to behave in an unusual fashion.
1920	John and Jim Dawson go into partnership as Dawson Brothers.
1925	Harry Dawson leaves Backridge and retires to Waddington. Annie Dawson joins the rest of the family at Bashall Hall.
1927	Felix Dawson dies in Australia. Jim Dawson has another breakdown in health.
1929	Jim Dawson has liaison with Lily Barker.
1930	Lily Barker leaves Clitheroe.
1931	Lily and Jack Lee join household at Bashall Hall. Jim Dawson is verbally abused by Harry Leeming at Red Pump Inn, Bashall Eaves.
1932	Tommy Kenyon taken on as farmhand at Bashall Hall.
January 1933	Tommy Simpson of Bashall Town Farm attacked at gates of Bashall Hall.
1933	Tommy Simpson and Tommy Kenyon brawl at Bashall Town.
10 April 1933	Death of Jim's older brother John Dawson at Bashall Hall.
July 1933	Poachers arrested in Bashall Eaves - case investigated by Superintendent Elliott of Settle.
Sept 1933	Boy dies as a result of falling from chestnut tree on Bashall Hall land.
Autumn 1933	Preparations for March lottery dinner at Edisford Bridge Hotel - raffling of prizes continues throughout the winter months.

1934

Jan/Feb	Jim Dawson begins to behave strangely and stays out at night again.
3 March	Jim does not turn up after the lottery dinner at the Edisford Bridge Hotel.
Early March	Stranger seen hanging around the Edisford Bridge Hotel. Slight quarrel between Jim Dawson and his nephews Jack Lee and Albert Pickles. Jim Dawson expresses worry about his brother John's will.
Mid March	Jim Dawson goes into partnership with Polly and Albert Pickles to trade as Dawson Brothers at Bashall Hall.
16/17 March	Jim Dawson present at Edisford Bridge Hotel in evening.

Sunday, 18th March 1934

7 p.m.	Jim leaves Bashall Hall for Edisford Bridge Hotel.
7.15 p.m.	Arrives at the public house.
8.10 p.m.	Buys drink for James Parkinson, a farm labourer.
8.50 p.m.	Some customers leave the pub for Clitheroe, some leave by car.
c. 9.00 p.m.	Jim buys a box of matches and leaves the pub. Albert Pickles retires to bed, shortly followed by Lily Lee. Jim seen walking home by Ernest Hodgson.
9.10 - 9.15 p.m.	Jim sees figure illuminated in oncoming car headlights at Brieryforth gate.
About 9.15 p.m.	Jim arrives at Brieryforth gate. 30 yards up Back Lane, hears click and feels sharp pain in right shoulder.
9.20 p.m.	Jim arrives home at Bashall Hall and enters kitchen. Jack Lee also enters kitchen. Polly Pickles gives Jim supper.
9.40 p.m.	Jim retires to bed, after sitting by fire for a few minutes.
c.10. 20 p.m.	Jack Lee joins his uncle Jim in their shared bedroom.
10.30 p.m.	Tommy Kenyon, the farmhand, returns home.
About 11.45 p.m.	Jim Dawson realises that he has been shot.

Monday, 19th March 1934

7.40 a.m.	Lily Lee enters bedroom to wake son Jack. Jim Dawson asks her to look at his back. Blood on sheets and under bed. Lily Lee calls in their sister Polly Pickles. Lily Lee notices tiny drops of blood at the top of the stairs. Doctor and police called.
10 - 11 a.m.	Doctor Cooper and P.C. Sheldon arrive at Bashall Hall.
Early afternoon	Jim Dawson and Lily Lee go to Blackburn by taxi. X-ray of Jim's back taken by Dr. Taylor at Preston New Road reveals large bullet lodged in his right armpit. Jim Dawson refuses medical treatment and returns to Bashall Hall.
4.15 p.m.	Inspector Elliott arrives from Settle and interviews Jim, who shows him the scene of the assault.

Tuesday, 20th March 1934

7 a.m.	Harold Newhouse arrives at Bashall Hall to help out.
Mid-day	Jim Dawson's brother Harry arrives at Bashall Hall and begs his brother to tell the police all he knows.

Afternoon   Dr. Cooper called out again as bullet wound deteriorating.
About 5 p.m.   Jim Dawson taken to Blackburn nursing home, Shear Bank Road, Blackburn where operation is performed to remove the bullet.

Wednesday, 21st March 1934

Jim Dawson 'as well as can be expected'.
Police take statements from all resident at Bashall Hall.

Thursday, 22nd March 1934

Time unknown   George Leach, assistant clerk to Blackburn Magistrates takes final statement from Jim Dawson at Blackburn nursing home.
3.30 p.m.   Jim Dawson dies of septicaemia.

APPENDIX 2

Postscript

Readers may like to acquaint themselves with the fate of some of the characters who found themselves caught up in the drama of Jim Dawson's murder. This is what happened to them next.

Lily and Jack Lee

Shortly after the death of Jim Dawson, his sister Lily Lee and her son Jack departed from Bashall Hall. Lily bought a house just outside the medieval village of Whalley about three miles from Bashall Eaves with money which she had inherited from a member of the Lee family. In 1943, Jack married Olive Hargreaves from Billington. Olive moved into the Whalley house with her new husband and mother-in-law. Jack and Olive had two daughters, Patricia Ann (in 1945) and Jennifer (in 1953). In 1956 or thereabouts, Lily Lee moved out of her Whalley house as it had become infested by a shrieking, asthmatic demon (that would be me) and at her age she couldn't stand it.

Lily therefore made an escape bid and moved in with her sisters Annie and Polly in Clitheroe and remained there until she became ill in 1960. She then returned briefly to her Whalley house where she died aged 76. Lily was buried in Mitton churchyard, with her infant son, Ronald. Her son Jack Lee spent most of his working life as office manager at C.W.S. Withgill Farm Estate, near Mitton. He is alive and kicking at 88 years of age and still lives in the Whalley house which his mother Lily bought in 1934.

Polly and Albert Pickles

After Jim's murder, his sister Polly and nephew Albert continued to live at Bashall Hall. Due to Albert's inexperience, it was decided that he should farm only that part of the Bashall Hall estate known as Bashall Hall Farm rather than the entire estate. Jim's brother Harry Dawson of Waddington came out of retirement to run the larger portion of the estate known as Bashall Farm. Albert died of colitis in 1952 at the early age of 40, having kept up the family tradition of refusing medical treatment until it was too late.

His mother Polly then left Bashall Hall and their part of the estate was subsequently taken over by their farmhand, Fred Pye. Polly spent a few weeks in Whalley with her sister Lily Lee and then moved in with her sister Annie in Clitheroe. A year later, Polly died of cancer at the age of 77. Polly and Albert Pickles are buried together in Mitton churchyard, not far from Jim Dawson.

Annie Dawson

When her sisters Polly and Lily died, Annie continued to live at Kirkmoor Road on her own. She never married. I remember Auntie Annie very well as we visited her regularly when I was young. My abiding memory is of her sitting in a beautiful rocking chair, which is now my own. I also remember as a child being fascinated by what appeared to be a large stuffed fish mounted on the wall of her immaculate living room. By 1971, when I was 18 and studying for my A Levels at Clitheroe Royal Grammar School For Girls, Annie's health had begun to fail and she moved into a flat in Waddington. Eventually my father brought her to Whalley for nursing care. I was interested to see the following entries in my 1971 diary:

Sunday 31st January, 1971

Got up about 12.45 again. Had dinner and did Latin unseen and history essay. Then dad told me about our family - people being murdered, people committing suicide, people going mad - what a lovely family history I have. Then drew a bit, had tea and read Dracula.

A couple of months later I recorded:

Thursday, 22nd April 1971

Auntie Annie died. She'd just had dinner and mum heard a thump and said to me, "It sounds like Auntie Annie's fallen." A few minutes later she came down saying, "She's dead." I had to go and ring for dad and Ken. Funeral arrangements - Maxwell is executer [sic] and me, dad and him went to look for the will. We took it to Uncle Harry. The funeral director rang up later to say Uncle Harry was making a fuss over which grave Auntie Annie is to be buried in. I got up and got books out of the room where Auntie Annie is. It scares me to have somebody dead in the same house. Couldn't sleep last night. Bad dreams. No pictures fell at Auntie Annie's which is the usual omen of death in our family*. None fell here either. Everything is upside down and mournful.

Annie Dawson was eventually buried in the same grave as her brothers Jim and John at Mitton on Monday, 26th April.

Harry Dawson

Jim's forceful brother Harry Dawson eventually handed over responsibility for his part of the Bashall Hall estate to his son Howard, who continued to farm it until the sale of the entire Bashall Hall estate in 1972. Harry died in 1976 and was buried at Waddington. Howard now lives at Low Moor in Clitheroe.

---

* My father informs me that it was only at Bashall Hall that falling pictures were a death omen for the family.

Bob Dawson

Bob Dawson, who had been so convinced that Jim's murder was due to a woman, opened his own ironmonger's shop in Parson Lane, Clitheroe in the late 1930s. Here he lived above the shop with his wife May and sons Maxwell and Charlie. As a child I remember watching Clitheroe's 1960 Torchlight Procession from the upstairs window of Uncle Bob's living room which overlooked Parson Lane. It provided an excellent vantage point, enabling us to look down upon all the strange floats* and banners wending their way past the castle, which looms over the steep little lane. When Bob Dawson died in 1965, his son Maxwell took over the business.

The relatively small ironmongers shop started by Bob Dawson is now located in King Street, Clitheroe and has grown into the substantial and up-market Dawson's Department Store, where it is possible to buy just about anything your house or garden might require. The premises have recently been extended further to house The Ethos Gallery selling local art and providing a picture-framing service. The store also boasts an elegant café and wine bar named Maxwell's, after Bob's son. The café lattes are excellent! The store is still run as a family concern by members of the Dawson family.

William Dawson

It is a relief to report that William Dawson, after a shaky start, lived happily ever after in Australia, where he had emigrated in 1909. Several dozen Aussie Dawsons now carry on the family name down under, and occasionally come over to visit. William himself died in 1967.

Tommy Kenyon

Tommy Kenyon eventually moved to Cardigan Street in Preston, but I have been unable to establish for how long he remained at Bashall Hall after the murder of Jim Dawson. I do not know what became of him after 1980 when we interviewed him in Preston.

Nancy Simpson

Nancy married a local lad who adored her and eventually moved to Salford, Manchester. She returned briefly to the area in 1979 when she and Tommy Kenyon were interviewed together at the Red Pump Inn in Bashall Eaves for the T.V. programme "The Village That Wouldn't Talk". What finally became of her I do not know.

---

* Including a beatnik float and The Gas Works Dalek!

The Ormerods of Bashall Hall Cottage

After the murder of Jim Dawson, things did not go at all well for the barrister and his family at Bashall Hall Cottage. The first unlucky accident involved their child who was severely burned in a too-hot bath. The poor thing was apparently lucky to escape with its life.

Close on the heels of this episode, the Clitheroe Advertiser and Times reported on October 5th 1934 that Mr. Ormerod himself had been severely injured at the Hall. At about eight o'clock at night there had been a deafening crash, as Bashall Hall's chimney collapsed. The bed on which Mr. Ormerod was lying was buried beneath 10 cwt of stones and plaster. The Ormerod's maid, Nancy Simpson, and neighbour Polly Pickles (who had heard the crash from next door) worked frantically to remove the debris. When the stones had been lifted away, Mr. Ormerod was found to have serious head and chest injuries. He was carried off by ambulance to his Blackburn house. Harry Dawson commented later that some of the stones which fell on the barrister weighed at least 20 lbs. The Ormerod family sensibly decided that the Bashall Hall air wasn't good for them and departed forthwith.

Bashall Hall

The Worsley-Taylor family decided to sell the Bashall Hall estate in 1972, along with Bashall Town Farm (where Tommy Simpson had lived and died). It was originally intended to sell the estate by auction. The sales particulars make interesting reading. By 1972, it seems that Bashall Hall itself was divided into three parts - the main part being the farmhouse where the Dawsons had lived, the second part being 'a great hall now in somewhat dilapidated condition which is in hand' and the third part (Bashall Hall Cottage) being 'a cottage let to the tenant of Bashall Farm for a farm worker' and which was originally the West Wing of the Hall. Bashall Hall Farm (rent £300) was tenanted by Fred Pye, and Harry Dawson was the tenant of Bashall Farm (rent £510).

Also included in the sale was Bashall Town Farm (rent £700), whose tenant in 1972 was Mr. G. Towler.

Harry Dawson originally expressed a wish to purchase Bashall Hall for his son Howard but eventually decided against it, as he had no wish to buy Bashall Town as well.

The auction of Bashall Hall and Bashall Town never took place. On Thursday November 2nd 1972 the following notice appeared in the Clitheroe Advertiser and Times:

> **A. W. WATTS & CO.**
> Harewood Lane
> Northallerton, Yorks, DL7 8BH
> TEL. 0609 2793
> AND AT BARNARD CASTLE AND YARM
>
> # Bashall Hall Estate
>
> This Estate has now been sold
> Privately and the Auction
> Sale arranged for
> November 7th
> at the Starkie Arms, Clitheroe
> HAS BEEN CANCELLED

The new owners of Bashall Hall were Mr. and Mrs. Barnes, who have lovingly restored the wonderful old building to all its former glory. It is now a beautiful and privately-owned family home.

Thus after more than two hundred years, the Dawson family connection with Bashall Hall was in 1972 finally severed once and for all.

Dawson Family Tree

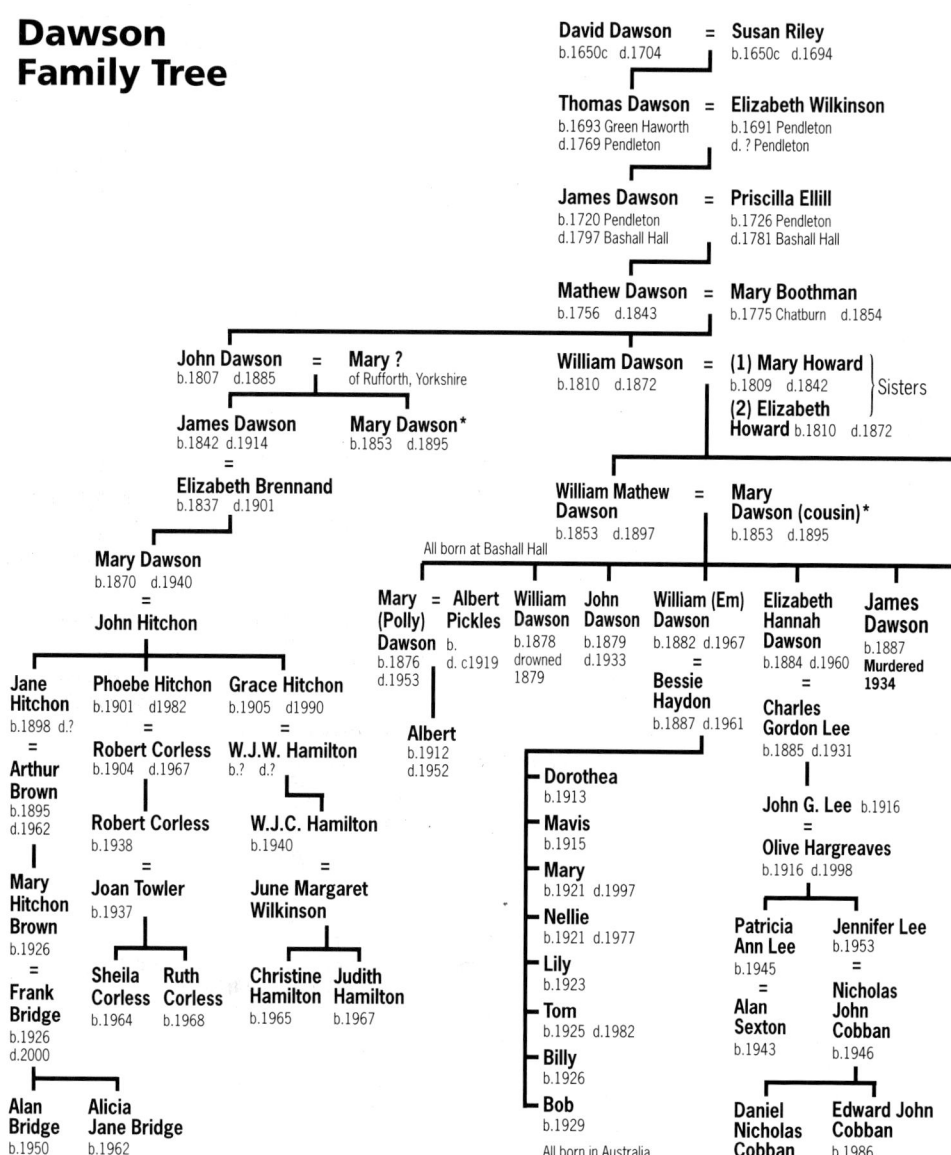

Key	
Em	Emigrated
=	Married to
c	Circa

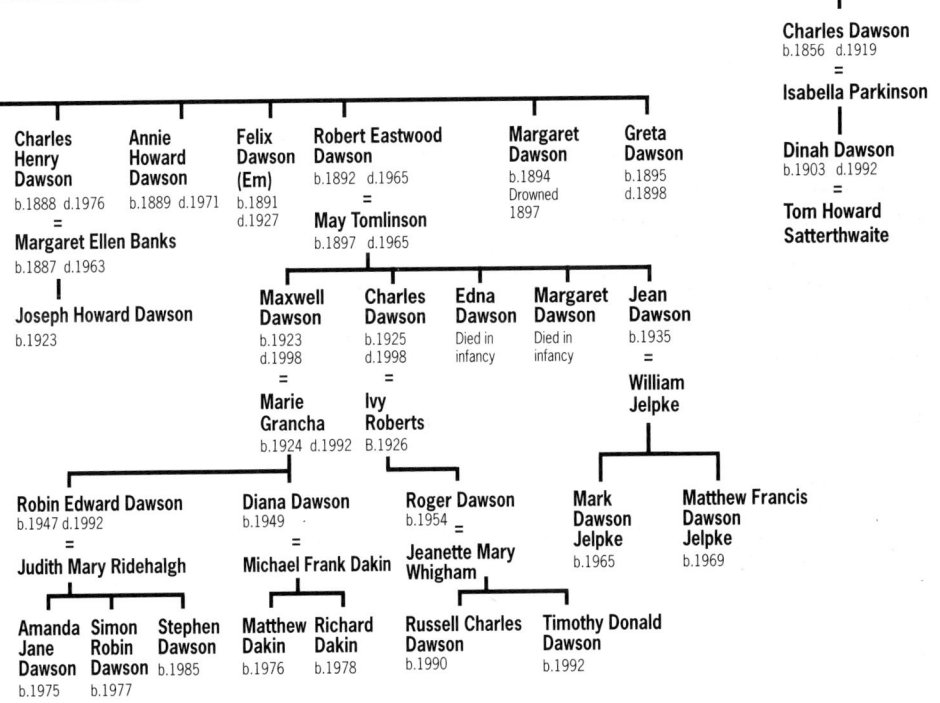

SOURCES

Abram, A., *History of Blackburn Town and Parish, 1888.*
Alderson, J., *A History of the West Riding Constabulary (1856 - 1968), 2001.*
Barrett's General and Commercial Directories of Blackburn and District
Brooks, David S., *Brungerley Hipping Stones, 1992.*
North Yorkshire Police, *Case File: The Murder of Jim Dawson 1934.*
Clitheroe Advertiser and Times
Clitheroe Library Archives
Cobban, N. J., *Personal notes*
Dawson, H., *Personal Memories*
Dixon, J. & P., *Journeys through Brigantia, Vol. 9, The Ribble Valley, 1993.*
Dobson, W., *Rambles round the Ribble, 1864.*
Dugdale, G., *Walks in Mysterious Lancashire, 1999.*
Eccles, W., *Personal Interview*
Entwistle, T. A., *Great Mitton, All Hallows, Where Rivers Meet, Vol. 1, No 1, Whalley and District Historical and Archaeological Society.*
Fielding, J.T., *A Record of Rambles, Historical Facts, Legends and Nature Notes, Volume 1 (1905) and Volume 2 (1906).*
Freethy, R., *Exploring Bowland and the Hodder, 1987.*
Greenwood, M., and Bolton, C., *Bolland Forest and the Hodder Valley, 2000.*
Hallam, Jack, *The Ghosts' Who's Who, 1977.*
Halliwell, Jo (Ed) *John Warkworth: A Chronicle of the First 13 Years of the reign of Edward IV, Camden Society 1839.*
Hastings, Macdonald, *The Other Mr. Churchill: A Biography of Robert Churchill, 1963.*
Hastings, Sir Max, *Personal Communications*
Haward, W. I., *Secret Rooms of North West England, 1964.*
Hey, D. (Ed.) *The Oxford Companion to Local and Family History, 1998.*
Holden, Sue, *Clitheroe Ablaze with Glory, 1999.*

James, M.R. (Ed.) *Henry VI: A reprint of John Blacman's Memoirs, 1919.*
Kenyon, T., *Personal Interview*
Lancashire Record Office, *Register of Electors, 1934.*
Langshaw, W., *Clitheroe's Thousand Years, circa 1952.*
Frankland, M., *Personal Interview*
Lee, J. G., *Personal Memories*
Lofthouse, J., *Lancashire's Fair Face, 1952. Three Rivers, 1946.*
Masters, D., *Personal Communication*
McNulty, Rev. J., *The Early History of the Parish of Mitton, 1951.*
Pevsner, N., *Buildings of England, 1969.*
Radio Times, *25th June, 1964.*
Ramsey, Sir James H., *Lancaster and York, 1399 - 1485, 1892.*
Royal Commission on the Historical Monuments of England, *Rural Houses of the Lancashire Pennines 1560 - 1760, 1985.*
Slack, M., *The Bridges of Lancashire and Yorkshire, 1986.*
Smith, Rev. R., *Ye Illustrated Chronicles of Craven, Yorkshire, undated.*
Spenceley, R. H., *Bashall, Where Rivers Meet, Vol. 2, No. 1, Whalley and District Historical and Archaeological Society*
Towler, G., *Personal Interview*
University of Boston: *Personal Communication*
University of Texas: *Personal Communication*
Victoria County History of the Counties of England: *A History of Lancashire, Vol. VI, 1911.*
Weeks, W. Self, *Some Legendary Stories and Folklore of the Clitheroe District, 1917. Further Legendary Stories and Folklore of the Clitheroe District, 1922.*
Whitaker, T. D., *A History of the Original Parish of Whalley and Honor of Clitheroe, 1872. The History and Antiquities of the Deanery of Craven in the County of York, Vols. 1 and 2, 1878.*
Whitaker, Terence W., *Lancashire Ghosts and Legends, 1980.*

The
Edisford
Bridge Inn
Clitheroe
Tel: 01200 422637

~Good Food~
~Riverside Location~
~Beer Garden~

OPENING HOURS
MON-SAT: 11 A.M.-11 P.M.
SUNDAY 12 A.M.-10.30 P.M.
FOOD SERVED
MON-THURS: 11.30 A.M. - 2 P.M.
FRI, SAT, SUN: 11.30 A.M. - 9 P.M.
(9.30 P.M. ON SATURDAY)

DAWSON'S

THE DEPARTMENT STORE

56 KING STREET, CLITHEROE
TEL: (01200) 425151

~COOKSHOP~SMALL ELECTRICALS~
~GARDENING~PAINTS~DIY~TOOLS~LINEN~
~GIFTS~LUGGAGE~HANDBAGS~COLLECTABLES~
~MOORCROFT~BEDEC~FINE ARTS~
~ROYAL CROWN DERBY~~

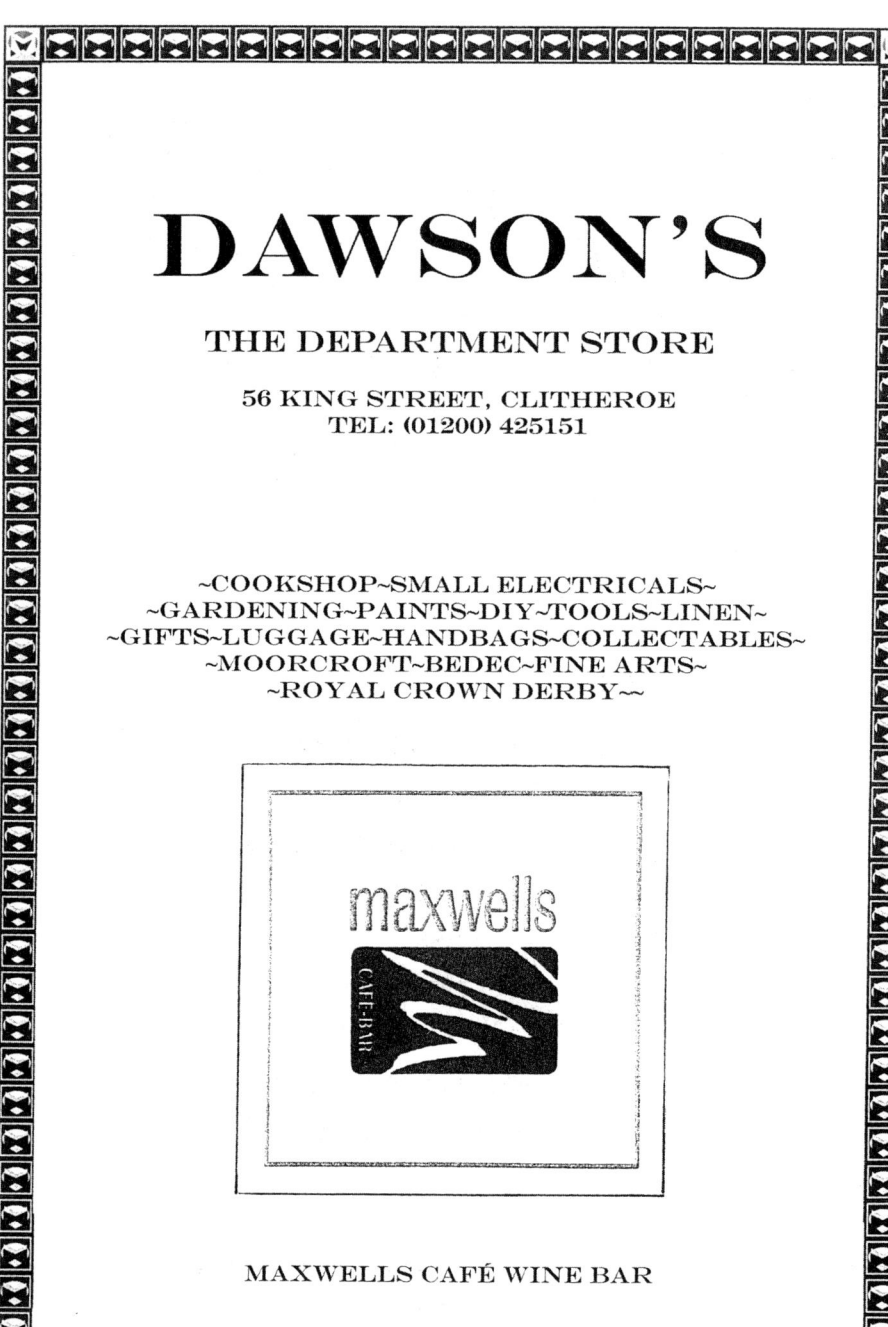

MAXWELLS CAFÉ WINE BAR

BASHALL BARN

Bashall Town, Clitheroe
Telephone 01200 428964
www.bashallbarn.co.uk

— Lancashire's Finest Foods & Gifts —

Organic & Speciality Meats
Cheese Store
Pickles, Preserves and Sauces
Ice Creams
Glass
Candles and other Craftware
Furniture and Art
Toys, Cuddlies and Puzzles
The Green Oak Café

Toilet, baby changing and stair lift facilities available
Easy Parking

Other Places to Visit

The Red Pump Inn
Bashall Eaves, Nr. Clitheroe
Tel: 01254 826227

The Punch Bowl Inn
Hurst Green, Lancashire
Tel: 01254 826678

Browsholme Hall
Near Clitheroe, Lancashire
Tel: 01254 428964

Stonyhurst College
Hurst Green, Lancashire
Tel: 01254 826345   www.stonyhurst.ac.uk

Whalley Abbey
Whalley, Lancashire
Tel: 01254 828400

Clitheroe Castle Museum
Clitheroe, Lancashire
Tel: 01200 424635   www.ribblevalley.gov.uk

Clitheroe Auction Mart
Lincoln Way, Clitheroe
Tel: 01200 423325

The Solberge Hall Hotel
Newby Wiske, N. Yorkshire
Tel: 01609 779191

For further information contact:
Clitheroe Tourist Information Centre, Market Place, Clitheroe
Tel: 01200 425566
tourism@ribblevalley.gov.uk

N.B. Bashall Hall is a privately-owned house and is not open to the general public. Please respect the privacy of its residents.